THE SALVATION OF THE GENTILES

Essays on the Acts of the Apostles

DOM JACQUES DUPONT, O.S.B.

translated by
John R. Keating, S.J.

PAULIST PRESS
New York/Ramsey/Toronto

Acknowledgements
All of the essays presented here were printed in the volume *Etudes sur les Actes des Apôtres*, Lectio Divina 45 (Paris: Editions du Cerf, 1967). They are listed here, following the order of the present translation, according to their title and location within the *Etudes*; and original publication data is also given for those essays which had previously been published elsewhere. Chapter I: "Le salut des Gentils et la signification théologique du Livre des Actes," *Etudes*, pp. 393-415, reprinted from *New Testament Studies* 6 (1959-1960), pp. 132-155. Chapter II: "La première Pentecôte chrétienne," *Etudes*, pp. 481-502, reprinted from *Assemblées du Seigneur*, no. 51, Bruges, 1963, pp. 39-62. Chapter III: "La conversion dans les Actes des Apôtres," *Etudes*, pp. 459-476, reprinted from *Lumière et Vie* 47 (1960), pp. 47-70. Chapter IV: "La communauté des biens aux premiers jours de l'Eglise," *Etudes*, pp. 503-519, not previously published. Chapter V: "L'interpretation des Psaumes dans les Actes des Apôtres," *Etudes*, pp. 283-307, reprinted from *Le Psautier. Ses origines. Ses problemes littéraires. Son influence. Etudes presentées aux XIIIe Journeés Bibliques de Louvain* (29-31 août 1960) (Orientalia et Biblical Lovaniensia, IV), Louvain, 1962, pp. 357-388. Chapter VI: 'L'utilisation apologétique de l'Ancien Testament dans les discours des Actes," *Etudes* pp. 245-282, reprinted from *Ephemerides Theologicae Lovanienses* 29 (1953) (=Analecta Lovaniensia Biblica et Orientalia, series 2, fasc. 40, Louvain and Bruges-Paris, 1953), pp. 298-327.

Library of Congress
Catalog Card Number: 78-65901

ISBN: 0-8091-2193-X

Published by Paulist Press
Editorial Office: 1865 Broadway, New York, N.Y. 10023
Business Office: 545 Island Road, Ramsey, N.J. 07446

Printed and bound in the
United States of America

Contents

Introduction

Students of the New Testament are indebted to Dom Jacques Dupont for contributions on a wide variety of topics, from his earliest work in Pauline literature to his most recent studies on the Beatitudes and the parables of Jesus. Among those contributions his studies on the Acts of the Apostles occupy a special place. In his Preface to the present volume, Dom Dupont tells us how he first came to study Acts and describes some of his earliest insights into its meaning. That book has continued to fascinate him, claiming a large share of his attention as researcher, writer and lecturer ever since.

Very little of Dupont's work has been translated to date into English, though there are signs, even aside from the present book, that the situation may be beginning to change. The lack of translations has been unfortunate, for Dupont, in addition to his qualities as a scholar, has a fine feeling for the religious meaning of the Scriptures and their relevance for Christian life. This makes his work of interest not only to specialists, who have access to it in French, but also to a wider circle of readers; some of it was originally addressed to non-specialist groups in Belgium and France, or later adapted for such groups. The essays on the Acts of the Apostles translated here all exemplify his skill at literary analysis of Scripture and exposition of its theological and spiritual content. We know that there is a receptive, ever increasing audience for such writing in the English-speaking world, and we welcome the opportunity to make a sampling of Dupont's essays available to those potential new readers.

But their biblical-theological content is not the only appeal in these essays. A quality I have personally admired in Dom Dupont, either while reading his writings or on the few occasions when I

1

have heard him lecture is his talent for drawing readers and listeners into his own *process of discovery.* His approach is thoroughly text-centered, and his explication of a text always exhibits a Gallic orderliness; even complex materials are organized with pedagogical skill and presented in clear, intelligible fashion. Dupont moves neatly from analysis to synthesis, from details to the whole. He builds an exposition slowly, taking as his starting point features of language, of structure, of symbolism, appealing along the way to instructive parallels, arriving finally at an understanding of the text as a unified theological statement. And as Dupont "unpacks" a text in this way, we share the excitement and suspense of the process; we experience along with him the revelation of its meaning.

The six essays selected for this collection have been edited with the interests of non-specialists in mind. They are reduced to uniform, non-technical format, without their original documentation, but publication data is supplied so that those who desire further information may be able to find it. On occasion, when it seemed possible to express a thought more clearly, Dupont's wording has been paraphrased, or divisions in the material more explicitly articulated; no further attention will be called to such slight changes which leave the substance of the essays unaffected. Repetition from one chapter to another, inevitable in a collection of this sort, has been allowed to stand, and presents several advantages. It enables a reader to read each chapter independently, without necessarily following their sequence in this volume. Further, when the same basic idea emerges in several contexts it is reinforced by virtue of the repetition, so that the reader may grasp it more easily and more accurately judge its importance.

Yet there is a certain naturalness to the order in which the essays are here arranged, and a certain logical flow of the material from the opening chapter to the closing ones. Hence a reader might profitably follow this sequence.

The lead essay sets the tone for the whole collection. In this chapter Dupont uncovers Luke's motive in writing the Acts of the Apostles, the theological vision which commands his work. This insight is basic, for it enables us to answer such questions as the following: Rather than being content just to tell the story of Jesus, like the other evangelists, why did Luke feel compelled to write the story of the early Church as well? Why is the apostle Paul the central figure in this story? Could the Christian Church have remained strictly Jewish, or was the mission to the Gentiles also a necessary item on Jesus' agenda as Messiah? In this first essay already sound the great themes that will recur in the chapters which follow: the universality of Jesus' messianic mission, the fulfillment of messianic prophecy, the need to reconcile continuity with a Jewish past and outreach to the world beyond Judaism, the tension between conformity and innovation in Christian experience. The concepts expressed in this essay are so fundamental in Dupont's view of Acts that he spontaneously returns to some of them in his own preface to this collection.

The second chapter invites us to a close guided study of a particular text, the Pentecost narrative, in the hope of discovering Luke's special personal point of view in composing this crucial episode. Some of the questions this chapter raises are: Why does Luke date the coming of the Spirit on a precise day, the Jewish feast of Pentecost? What are we to make of the pyrotechnics and the extraordinary sound-effects? Is that curious phenomenon, "speaking in other tongues," related to spiritual gifts experienced elsewhere in the early Church or in our contemporary charismatic movement? And, finally, how is this dramatic event integrated into Luke's theology of Christian mission? This chapter is a fine example of the art of the exegetical essay, a medium in which Dupont is a master. Readers will find that the application of his method to the Pentecost narrative yields results that are rich and rewarding indeed.

The following two chapters deal with themes from Acts which help us to appreciate what it meant to be Christian in the first century, from the viewpoint both of the individual and of the community. The chapter on conversion reveals how early Christians experienced the process of leaving their old lives behind and embarking upon a new one, and how they understood this experience theologically. Dupont illuminates the relation between individual change of life and the resurrection, the central event in Christian faith-awareness: conversion, too, is an Easter experience. The theology of conversion he develops helps us to understand similar sudden changes of life in later generations. It also sheds light on the continuing process of conversion that marks our own existence, our Christian journey, until the consummation.

The fourth chapter investigates the communitarian dimension of early Christian life, especially as reflected within the "summaries" in Acts. Do these passages establish a primitive communism among the first Christians, as is often supposed, or furnish evidence that they consciously pursued poverty as an ideal? Dupont attempts to define Christian practice in the sharing of wealth as accurately as possible, and determines, by consideration of possible parallels and sources of influence, the origin and theoretical significance of that practice. He detects in Luke's text a mingling of various cultural currents, a fusion of influences from both biblical thought and popular Hellenistic philosophy. He concludes that Luke's descriptions of sharing of wealth in the primitive community are shaped less by economic or ascetical theories than they are by the Christian ideal of charity; at the same time they reflect the Greek ideal of equality among friends, so that they would spontaneously remind his first readers of the concept of friendship prevalent in their own culture.

The final two essays are complementary. They treat for its own sake a theme which gets only passing attention in the foregoing studies: the fulfillment of Old Testament prophecy. The fifth chapter discusses in some detail individual passages from the psalms which are interpreted messianically in early Christian preaching. The sixth chapter encompasses a wider range of material, surveying all major Old Testament texts, from the Pentateuch and the prophets as well as from the psalms, that are exploited for apologetic purposes within the speeches in Acts. These two essays, taken together, provide an excellent introduction to an important, though insufficiently understood, matter: the nature of Old Testament interpretation as practiced in the early Church. As Dupont leads us from example to example, presuppositions come to light and hermeneutical patterns emerge, so that we acquire a feeling for the method and insight into how it works. These studies also help us to distinguish early Christian exegesis, which moves entirely within faith, from the kind of historico-critical exegesis of a text, with concern for its original literal sense, such as we are in a position to practice in modern times. Each of these approaches operates within its own conventions and is valid in its own domain; problems can arise for us only when the distinction between the methods is confused or when we opt for one to the exclusion of the other. Finally, Dupont suggests some ways in which early Christian methods of interpretation retain their relevance for us today, and indicates the special quality that the psalms have as prayer when they are prayed within the Christian community.

Two remarks about the translation are in order. We wish to thank Fr. Joseph A. Donceel, S.J. for preparing a preliminary draft in the latter part of 1977. The text here published, a very extensive revision of that draft in the interests of English idiom and exegetical precision, is substantially a new product, for which the editor of this volume bears sole responsibility. Citations from ancient texts, both biblical and extra-biblical, have been translated directly from Dupont's French version or, in cases where he cites the original, directly from the Greek or Latin. One exception to this rule occurs in the fifth chapter where it seemed useful to insert citations of psalm passages which Dupont discussed in some detail; the text employed in those inserted passages is the Revised Standard Version, even where that is not explicitly noted.

We hope that these essays, appearing now in a new language and in more popular form, will help to make the Acts of the Apostles better known, revealing unsuspected depths within its theology and surprising relevance for contemporary Christian life. We hope, too, that through them many new readers will make the acquaintance of Dom Dupont, an exegete of rare gifts, who can open our minds to the Scriptures and teach us to read them with fresh eyes.

Berkeley, California
Pentecost, 1978

John R. Keating, S.J.

Author's Preface

My earliest exegetical labors, under the direction of Lucien Cerfaux at the University of Louvain from 1942 to 1949, were devoted to the letters of St. Paul. But once that work was completed, Msgr. Cerfaux invited me to collaborate with him on research he was doing into the Acts of the Apostles; that was the beginning of a lasting interest for me, one which would lead me in time to the publication of a series of studies on Acts which has not yet come to an end. I am quite pleased, therefore, that Fr. John Keating has now undertaken the task of making a number of those studies available to English-speaking readers, and I would like to express my sincerest gratitude to him.

In my own personal experience, the Acts of the Apostles was the bridge I crossed in moving from the letters of Paul to the Gospels. It did not take me long to realize that I could not understand Acts apart from the Gospel of Luke, since the third Gospel and Acts are two inseparable parts of Luke's single work dedicated "To Theophilus." And the study of Luke's Gospel naturally led me to the other Synoptics as well, for how could I succeed in understanding Luke without comparing his version of the Gospel with the parallels in Mark and Matthew?

My discovery that Acts is a connecting link between the epistles and the story of Jesus' ministry squares quite well, I think, with Luke's own purpose in writing his second volume. The Church to which Luke belonged already felt at a certain distance from its roots. Its identity was not always obvious, nor continuity with its past keenly felt. Was there any clear connection between the little group of disciples which Jesus had gathered around himself or that first community which used to gather regularly in the temple at Jerusalem and those many Christian "cells" scattered by Luke's

7

time all over the Roman Empire, composed mostly of converted pagans and estranged from a Judaism now centered in its synagogues? One thing Luke hoped to accomplish in writing the Acts of the Apostles was to bridge the gap between those increasingly remote origins of the Christian movement and the reality of his Church at the close of the first century—which already exhibited, in fact, the characteristic features of the Church we know today.

There are several reasons why Acts is able to function as a connecting link between the Church at its starting point and the Church as it later came to be. The first is that the story Acts tells flows directly (whether we consider it merely from a narrative viewpoint or, even more significantly, from a theological one) out of the final episode in Luke's Gospel. The point of that finale is to establish that the Old Testament promises find their fulfillment in Jesus. The risen Jesus explains that personally to his disciples on Easter evening when he declares, "This is what is written [in the Scriptures]: that the Christ would have to suffer, that he would rise from the dead on the third day, and that in his name repentance for the remission of sins would be proclaimed to all nations, beginning from Jerusalem." This same idea is expressed also in Acts, for instance in Paul's final full-length statement, his speech before Agrippa, which he concludes in this way: "With the help I have received from God up to this very day, I stand and give witness before great and small, saying nothing but what the prophets and Moses predicted would happen, namely: that the Christ would have to suffer, and that, as the first to rise from the dead, he would announce the light to the [Jewish] people and the [pagan] nations." Both of these statements culminate in references to the non-Jewish nations and agree that the Messiah, as an integral part of his mission, must bring God's salvation to the Gentile world.

The finale of his Gospel clearly implies a conviction on the part of its author that the story of Jesus will not have been completely told until Jesus is shown to have accomplished his mission in its entirety, and the final part of Jesus' program is what the story of Acts is all about. For it is in the missionary preaching of the Church among the nations that Jesus' mission is brought to completion and Old Testament promises finally fulfilled. Thus Luke does not consider Jesus' story finished in his Gospel; Acts, the sequel to the Gospel, is still part of the Jesus story. The believer who grasps the point of Acts recognizes Jesus himself working within his witnesses, for he realizes that the actions and accomplishments of the apostles, as Acts recounts them for us, are the continuation of Jesus' own messianic activity.

There is also another way in which Acts reflects the transition from the earliest conditions of the Church to conditions in Luke's own time. Everyone knows that the first generation of Christians experienced a gradually widening rift between the Church and the synagogue which led eventually to complete separation. One of Luke's concerns is obviously to demonstrate that throughout that period of profound change the Christian community remained faithful to its origins. Therefore he emphasizes that the transformation of the original group of disciples into a universal Church has been predicted beforehand by the Law and the prophets, that it corresponds to the intention of the risen Jesus, and that it has happened under the direct guidance of God and his Spirit. If infidelity played a part in the separation, it was the infidelity of the Jewish leadership, and Acts places the responsibility squarely on their shoulders. They reject the testimony both of the Scriptures and of the "signs" that God works through the preachers of the Gospel. Not satisfied with rejecting the message of salvation, they do not even hesitate to resort to violence, persecuting the disciples and putting them to death, as they have already done to the Master; they exclude themselves from the people of God at the very moment God has chosen to create a people for himself from all the nations of the world.

The upheaval that the first generation of Christians lived through cannot but interest Christians of today who have the impression that everything, both in our world and in our Church, is undergoing change. The history which the Acts of the Apostles narrates provides us with a model that we can imitate, because it teaches us what form fidelity to Jesus and his Gospel must take in times of change. Acts does not encourage fruitless clinging to a past which may have been very beautiful in its time but which is really gone. It does inspire in us a concern to live the spirit of Jesus and his message in a present which is always new, and a conviction that the same Spirit Jesus sent upon his apostles continues to be active in the Church of our day.

Ottignies, Belgium   Jacques Dupont, O.S.B.
March 28, 1978

The Salvation of the Gentiles
and the
Theological Significance of Acts

St. Luke considered it necessary to add to the Gospel story, as conceived by the primitive Church and committed to writing by Mark, the narratives that make up the second book of his work "To Theophilus." What purpose lay behind this innovation? Though the question is still strongly debated, commentators generally agree that his intention was not purely historical. The disinterested pleasure of retracing in an objective study the origins of the Christian movement would not have been sufficient to account for his work. There must have been other motives that impelled Luke to undertake the composition of the Acts of the Apostles and that led him to publish the finished book.

Some commentators stress apologetic motives. Luke is writing for Theophilus, a pagan officeholder, and desires to address through him pagan readers capable of influencing public opinion. In this way the author of Acts attempts to defend Christianity against the charges which are circulating against it and to show that the new religion, as the lawful heir of Judaism, is entitled to the privileges enjoyed by the religion of Israel. Some conjecture that the occasion may have been a more specific situation—for example, that Luke is writing what amounts to an *apologia* in defense of Paul, in the hope of influencing in his favor the verdict of the imperial court.

Other interpreters judge that the author of Acts intends his book for Christian readers, and they emphasize its didactic character. Hardly anyone today would subscribe to the theory of the nineteenth-century Tübingen school, which held that Acts was composed for the purpose of erasing all traces of the antagonism that existed back in the beginning between two conflicting concepts of Christianity, that of Peter on the one hand and of Paul on the other. Nowadays Luke's work is more generally considered as catechesis, intended to complete the religious instruction of believers.

A number of authors, however, refuse to choose between apologetic and didactic motives behind Acts, for they believe that diverse motives, far from being mutually exclusive, could quite easily have co-existed in Luke's mind, each influencing in its own way and to its own degree the final shape of his work.

It is not our intention to reopen this question in its entirety, nor to trace all of its ramifications afresh. Our own purpose in the present essay is a more modest one: it is to cull and to present some of the clues which Luke left within his work, some of the pointers by means of which he seems to have wanted to help his readers discover the meaning he himself saw in the story he was telling.

Although we cannot analyze at any great length the arrangement Luke has imposed on his materials, it is evident that the structure of any work may furnish very valuable information about the intention of its author, provided we can grasp the precise significance of that structure. In Luke's case a geographical outline supplies him with the overall framework of his narratives. Thus in his first volume, Luke relates first of all Jesus' ministry in Galilee, then his journey from Galilee to Jerusalem, and finally the events in Jerusalem. The arrangement is rather artificial. The Galilee section acquires its geographical homogeneity only as a result of omissions and transpositions; the journey narrative owes its unity not to any common element in its contents, but only to three explicit reminders of the journey inserted amid the otherwise miscellaneous stories gathered together into this section (9:51; 13:22; 17:11); and in the finale of the Gospel, the setting can be restricted to Jerusalem only by deliberately eliminating every mention of appearances in Galilee.

The outline of Luke's second volume is roughly indicated in Acts 1:8: "You will be my witnesses in Jerusalem, in the whole of Judea and Samaria, and to the ends of the earth." The opening chapters of Acts do in fact deal with the preaching of the apostles in Jerusalem. A second section shows the expansion of their preaching into Samaria, to the coastal plain, and finally its implantation in Antioch. Antioch in turn becomes the starting point for Paul's missions throughout the Aegean. From 19:21 onward the outlook turns toward Rome, and the reader is reminded of this orientation at 23:11 and 27:24. Once Rome is reached, the book comes to a rapid conclusion.

This outline is admittedly geographical, but it has more than geographical significance. Jerusalem has an exceptional theological importance in Luke's thinking, for it is the Holy City, in which the prophecies are to be fulfilled. Likewise the expansion of Christianity is not a merely geographic phenomenon. As Christianity extends by progressive stages from Jerusalem to Rome, it also passes from the Jewish world to the Gentile world, and it is precisely that aspect of the expansion which interests Luke. Hence he repeatedly emphasizes the fact that the evangelization of the Gentiles is not the result of fortuitous circumstances. Rather the Gentile mission is willed by God, and it realizes the prophetic promises that the Messiah would bring salvation to the pagan nations; thus it is part and parcel of the program assigned to the Christ by the Scriptures. That is the reason why Luke decided to add the story of the apostolic missions to his narrative about Jesus, for without those missions the work of salvation described in the messianic prophecies would not be complete. The history he relates in Acts, therefore, appears to be a history charged with theological meaning.

This is the point we would like to establish. And in order to demonstrate it, we shall appeal to those passages in which Luke is most likely to have given us clues to his own intention in writing. We shall focus our attention on the introductions, and even more on the conclusions, of Luke's two-volume work. For these are passages in which, as we shall see, Luke is always careful to remind his readers of his theological perspective and thus to reveal to them the deepest significance of the history he is recounting.

I. ENDINGS AND BEGINNINGS

The Conclusion of Acts and the Introduction to the Gospel

The finale of each of the volumes in Luke's work "To Theophilus" exhibits similar literary features. In each case there is an extremely solemn conclusion: in the Gospel this consists of a declaration by the risen Jesus (Luke 24:44-49); in Acts it is a declaration by Paul, the prisoner (Acts 28:25-28). And this conclusion is followed in each case by a brief epilogue, an editorial comment. The final remark in the Gospel (Luke 24:50-53) describes the attitude of the apostles as they wait for the coming of the Spirit, and the notes of joy and piety that are struck here link the end of the first volume with the beginning of the second. The epilogue of Acts (28:20-31) characterizes the situation of Paul during his imprisonment in Rome 'and ends the work on a note of triumph. These epilogues conclude their respective works with an edifying touch, quite in Luke's manner, but the final editorial remarks are less significant than the great declarations by Jesus and Paul which precede them, and in which, we believe, the proper conclusion of each work is to be found. At present we shall consider the conclusion of Acts, and then in the following section the conclusion to Luke's Gospel.

Paul's declaration to the Jews of Rome consists essentially of a long quotation from Isaiah 6:9-10. The apostle remarks that his mission, like that of the prophet, results in the blindness of a people lacking in spiritual intelligence and unable to understand the necessity of conversion (Acts 28:25-27). Then he adds, and this is really the climax of the conclusion: "Be it known, therefore, that this salvation of God has been sent to the Gentiles; they at least will listen to it" (v. 28). The message of salvation, rejected by the people of Israel, will now be carried to the pagan nations, to the Gentiles. To designate the message of salvation, Paul uses the expression "this salvation of God" (*touto to soterion tou theou*) which does not come from the Isaiah citation. To grasp the meaning of this expression, it will be useful for us to compare the end of Acts with the beginning of Luke's Gospel.

In the thinking of the primitive Church the Gospel begins with the baptism of John the Baptist. On this point Mark has remained faithful to the tradition. Though the other evangelists feel a need to carry their stories further back in time (John by composing his prologue, Matthew and Luke by describing the circumstances of Jesus' birth), yet they all realize equally well, and Luke even more obviously than the others, that the ministry of John the Baptist constitutes the real "beginning of the Gospel." Luke reminds us of this on two occasions in Acts: at the election of Matthias (1:22), and in Peter's recapitulation of the life of Jesus (10:37; cf. 1:1). And in his Gospel, after the infancy narrative which is a long preamble, Luke seems to have wanted to highlight the decisive beginning by a very solemn introduction. He begins by synchronizing the vocation of John the Baptist with events of contemporary secular history (Luke 3:1-2), and then proceeds to cite at length a passage from Isaiah (40:3-5; Luke 3:4-6) that puts his narrative in theological perspective. This quotation from Isaiah merits our closer attention.

Use of Isaiah 40:3 is admittedly not a Lucan innovation. The same text is cited at the same place in Mark (1:3) and in Matthew (3:3), and all three Synoptics present the text in the same form: "The voice of one crying in the wilderness, 'Prepare the way of the Lord, make his paths straight.' " The language here differs slightly from the original. The Massoretic text and the Septuagint both read: "make smooth the paths of our God," and the Targum interprets: "make smooth the paths before the community of our God." The Synoptics clearly speak not of God's paths, but of Jesus' paths, and the change is obviously deliberate. They interpret Isaiah's text christologically, so that John the Baptist is conceived as preparing the coming not of God himself, the Father, but of the Christ; he is the "Lord" whose paths are to be made straight. Thus in citing Isaiah 40:3 Luke is merely following a well-established tradition, and not expressing a fresh personal viewpoint.

On the other hand, Luke is the only one of the Synoptics who continues the quotation from Isaiah down as far as verse 5. In doing this Luke proceeds on his own, and thus gives us insight into his personal view of the history that is beginning here. Verse 5 reads: "And all flesh will see the salvation of God" (*to soterion tou theou*). The vocabulary here is also Lucan in a certain sense. When speaking of "salvation" the New Testament normally employs the feminine noun (*soteria*) rather than the possible alternative neuter form (*soterion*). But there are, nonetheless, four instances of the use of this neuter form in the New Testament; of these instances one is found in Ephesians 2:3, but all the others are in the writings of Luke: Luke 2:30 (a probable allusion to Isaiah 40:5), Luke 3:6 (a direct citation of Isaiah 40:5), and Acts 28:28 (the passage with which our consideration in this section began).

Luke is the only evangelist, therefore, who continues the traditional quotation from Isaiah 40 at this point in his Gospel up to the words, "And all flesh will see the salvation of God." Similarly Luke is the only evangelist who continues the Gospel story by going on to narrate the missions of the apostles. So in concluding his second volume with the statement that "this salvation of God" has been sent "to the pagan nations" (Acts 28:28), Luke seems to be inviting us to recall the allusion early in his first volume to "the salvation of God" which, according to Isaiah, was to be revealed "to all flesh" (Luke 3:5). The expression "to all flesh" here must surely mean for Luke "to the Gentiles as well as to the Jews."

By thus placing Isaiah 40:5 at the beginning of his Gospel story, and also drawing the conclusion of Acts from words that remind us of this same text, Luke betrays his strong interest in the idea that the salvation of God is manifested to all men. It seems reasonable to consider that interest one of the keys to his work: the history Luke wishes to trace is the history of the revelation of God's salvation for all flesh.

If this bit of evidence stood in isolation, we would have to be cautious not to exaggerate its importance as a factor in the author's thinking. But, as we shall see, other features also suggest that Luke attributes to the story he tells precisely the significance that we have just suggested.

The Conclusion of the Gospel
and the Introduction to Acts

Since Luke's work is divided into two volumes, we might look for signs of his purpose elsewhere than in the introduction and conclusion to the whole work. We might also take a close look at the points of transition: the conclusion to the first volume and the introduction to the second. And when we compare these passages, we discover that as a matter of fact there is a close relationship between them, and that they shed mutual light upon one another.

The conclusion of the Gospel, as we have already noted, consists of a declaration by Jesus; specifically, it contains a set of instructions which the risen Jesus gives his apostles before leaving them (Luke 24:44-49). Jesus first of all leads them to an understanding of the Scriptures: the Scriptures speak of himself, and they

must be fulfilled. He reduces the teaching of the messianic prophecies to three points:

> Thus it was written (1) that the Christ had to suffer (2) and to rise
> from the dead on the third day, (3) and that in his name repentance
> unto remission of sins should be preached to all nations, beginning
> from Jerusalem (vv. 46-47).

After that, Jesus gives the apostles, the witnesses of these things,
the command to wait in Jerusalem for the coming of the Holy
Spirit (vv. 48-49).

Since Jesus' explanations in verses 46-47 are based on Scripture, it is not surprising that the expressions he chooses to speak of
the passion and resurrection bring to mind precise Old Testament
texts, such as Isaiah 53:4 and Hosea 6:2. But it does not seem
possible, on the other hand, to connect with any definite Scripture
texts what Jesus says of the message of *metanoia* to be proclaimed
to all nations beginning from Jerusalem. This statement appears to
be simply an outline of the program that will be realized as the
story of Acts unfolds.

In the prologue to Acts Luke addresses Theophilus, to whom
his double-volume work is dedicated. He starts, as is customary, by
summarizing the content of his first volume, the Gospel, and we
should normally expect him at this point to announce the subject
matter of the second volume as well. But he gets so carried away by
the memory of earlier events that he omits in the opening verses
any reference to the subject matter of the new volume that is
beginning. Luke eventually compensates, however, for this breach
of literary convention, and he does so by letting Jesus himself
sketch the program for the Book of Acts in his final words to the
apostles:

> You shall receive a power, that of the Holy Spirit who will come
> down upon you, and then you shall be my witnesses in Jerusalem, in
> all Judea and Samaria, and as far as the ends of the earth (1:8).

This verse traces the great stages in the expansion of the apostolic
message and provides the general outline within which Luke orga-
nizes his narrative.

When we compare the introduction of Acts with the end of Luke's Gospel, we notice that Acts is quite detailed. It distinguishes not just two stages in the apostolic preaching ("all nations, beginning from Jerusalem"), but four phases: Jerusalem, Judea, Samaria, the ends of the earth. Of the four entries on this list, the first three are quite clear, and obviously refer to definite geographical locations. But the same cannot be said of the final item, "the ends of the earth." Though it is commonly supposed that Luke has a definite place in mind, and is referring in fact to Rome, where the story of Acts comes to an end, this expression is hardly a clear and obvious way of referring to Rome. This turn of phrase might, of course, seem logical in the language and from the point of view of the Jews in Palestine. But it is quite curious to hear Luke, a citizen of the Roman Empire, using that expression while speaking to Theophilus and other Graeco-Roman readers; from their point of view it is not at all natural to describe the Gospel as reaching the "ends of the earth" once it has arrived in Rome.

The phrase "the ends of the earth" recurs at the conclusion of Paul's first missionary discourse in Acts. This other passage will help us understand why Luke uses the expression in 1:8 even though its meaning might not be immediately clear to his Gentile readers. The ending of Paul's speech in the synagogue at Antioch in Pisidia strongly resembles his final declaration to the Jews of Rome which constitutes the ending of Acts, and the repetition of the same idea in both places is a sign of the importance Luke must attribute to it. At Antioch in Pisidia, as in Rome, Paul begins with a warning drawn from a prophetic text, and the quotation of Habakkuk 1:5 functions in Acts 13:41 in the same way as the quotation from Isaiah 6:9-10 in Acts 28:26-27. Paul then goes on to announce that he is going to turn to the Gentiles, and at this point he refers, more explicitly than in Acts 28:28, to a passage from Isaiah (49:6):

> It was necessary to announce the word of God first of all to you. But since you reject it and do not consider yourselves worthy of eternal life, for this reason we are turning toward the Gentiles. For this is the mandate that the Lord gave me: "I have established you as a light to the Gentiles [the pagan nations], so that you may carry salvation to the ends of the earth" (13:46-47).

This text shows that the expression "to the ends of the earth" is not to be taken in a purely geographic sense. In contrast to

Jerusalem, the "city of the great king" and center of the worship of the true God, the ends of the earth represent the pagan nations. Hence the parallelism: "I have established you as a light *to the* [pagan] *nations,* so that you may carry salvation *to the ends of the earth.*" This language, which adopts an essentially religious point of view, permits us also to grasp the concrete equivalence between the proclamation of the message "to all [pagan] nations" (Luke 24:47) and the witnessing of the apostles "to the ends of the earth" (Acts 1:8). The expansion of Christianity "to the ends of the earth" is not a merely geographic movement, but involves a passage out of the Jewish world into the Gentile world. So Rome, as the capital of the pagan world, is really situated "at the ends of the earth," but the reasoning implicit in this expression is more religious than geographic.

Although it is less clear than the phrase "to all the nations" of Luke 24:47, the expression "unto the ends of the earth" in Acts 1:8 has the advantage of being more theological. The allusion to Scripture that we might expect in Luke 24:47 we find in fact in Acts 1:8, and the text of Isaiah 49:6 which is echoed there reveals the full significance of the expression "to the ends of the earth." If the message is to extend that far, then it must not only be preached everywhere, but it must above all be preached to the Gentiles. And this is required in order that the messianic prophecies may be fulfilled in their entirety. For the passion and resurrection of Jesus do not constitute the entire work of the Messiah. For the complete accomplishment of that work, it is necessary that Paul announce salvation to the Gentiles and carry the Gospel message to Rome, the city that rules the nations. In that sense the narrative of Acts is the necessary complement of the Gospel story: the movement of Christianity from Jerusalem to the ends of the earth completes the realization of the program assigned to the Christ by the messianic prophecies.

II. JESUS, PETER, AND CORNELIUS

The attempt to explain the introduction to Acts led us in the previous section to Paul's inaugural discourse in Acts 13, and this in turn gave us the opportunity to notice the striking resemblance between Paul's final statement to the Jews of Antioch in Pisidia and his declaration to the Jews of Rome at the end of the book. These connections give us some idea of the importance that Luke attaches to Paul's inaugural discourse: it is a genuine model of Paul's preaching to the Jews, ending as it does with the warning that, after announcing the message to the Jews, he would turn to the Gentiles so that the prophecies might be fulfilled.

Features we have observed in this first missionary speech of Paul suggest that we should also take a look at some other programmatic discourses by means of which Luke tries to give an overall view of the teaching of his main figures. In this section, therefore, we shall consider the inaugural discourse of Jesus in the synagogue at Nazareth and Peter's inaugural on Pentecost day, and we shall notice that the endings of these two speeches resemble each other in a significant way and that they also remind us of the conclusions of Luke's Gospel and of Acts. After that we shall round out this section by comparing Peter's inaugural remarks at Pentecost with his final statements before leaving the scene in Acts.

Jesus' Speech at Nazareth
and Peter's Speech at Pentecost

Luke is not the only author to have thought of placing a programmatic discourse on Jesus' lips at the start of his ministry. In Matthew's Gospel the Sermon on the Mount fulfills precisely this function. Prior to the Sermon on the Mount, Matthew gives his readers only the minimal information they need in order to understand the situation, deliberately postponing until a later point in his Gospel most of the episodes that Mark places right at the beginning of Jesus' Galilean ministry. Further, Matthew expands the version of the Sermon which came to him from earlier tradition, adding to it a great deal of material drawn from other contexts. Owing to these editorial modifications, the Sermon on the Mount constitutes in Matthew a rather complete picture of the ideal of religious life proposed by Jesus.

In Luke's Gospel, the Sermon on the Plain comes at a later point in the story (6:20-49) and has less importance from the viewpoint of narrative structure. The function of a programmatic discourse is fulfilled instead by Jesus' speech in the synagogue at Nazareth (4:16-30). The placing of this speech involves certain transpositions similar to those made by Matthew. For instance, it is necessary for Luke to anticipate an episode that comes much later in Mark (6:1-6) and in Matthew (13:54-58). Yet Luke makes no attempt to conceal his alterations in chronology, since he lets stand a remark indicating that Jesus has already exercised his ministry in Capernaum: "All that we have heard of as done in Capernaum, do here in your own country likewise" (4:23). Furthermore, Luke fills out Mark's data about Jesus' preaching in Nazareth with fresh details of his own, details which are quite unlikely to have had any relation originally with the present Lucan context. In a word, the position that Luke assigns to the Nazareth episode in his Gospel and the elaborate development he gives it reveal his intention to highlight this event and Jesus' statements on this occasion. The importance he attributes to this passage suggests that it may be especially significant for an understanding of his work as a whole.

Jesus' speech opens with a messianic declaration. After reading the oracle from Isaiah 61:1-2, "The Spirit of the Lord is upon me; he has anointed me; he has sent me to bring Good News to the poor," Jesus asserts that Isaiah's prophecy has already been fulfilled. He thus presents himself openly as the Messiah, the Savior of the unfortunate, foretold by the prophet. The people of Nazareth discuss his claim but do not believe it; their attitude bears a striking resemblance to that of the Jews in Acts who refuse to accept Paul's message, whether they be in Antioch or Corinth or Rome. Jesus then speaks again, referring to two incidents recorded in the Book of Kings: the prophet Elijah's bestowing God's favor upon a widow in Sarepta in the territory of Sidon (1 Kings 17), and the prophet Elisha's healing Naaman the Syrian of leprosy (2 Kings 5). Though there were many widows and lepers within Israel itself, God's favors in these cases were given to outsiders.

What is the point of these remarks by Jesus? Their purpose in the immediate context is quite clear: in response to the jealousy of his fellow townsmen over the miracles he has performed in Capernaum, Jesus appeals to the example of Elijah and Elisha who also wrought miracles on behalf of foreigners. Clearly, however, the point at issue is wider than the particular situation at Nazareth, and in the general context of Luke's work Jesus' argument obviously acquires a deeper significance. The contrast between Israel on the one hand and a Syrian or a Phoenician on the other is to be understood, of course, in function of the antithesis between Israel and the Gentiles. The example of Elijah and Elisha bestowing God's favors upon pagans gives us an intimation that the message of salvation, rejected by Israel as it is by Jesus' compatriots, will pass to the Gentiles. Thus the episode in Nazareth is a portent of what will happen in Antioch of Pisidia and in Rome, and Paul's behavior in turning to the Gentiles is justified beforehand by the action of Elijah and Elisha of old.

Let us turn now to Peter's inaugural address (Acts 2:14-40). It is a speech delivered before the crowd brought together by the Pentecost miracle, a crowd composed of "Jews and proselytes" (v. 11), of "devout men from all the nations under heaven" (v. 5). It is too early for Peter to speak directly to pagans at this point in the story. Yet Luke obviously enjoys enumerating the nations that are represented in the crowd: "Parthians, Medes and Elamites, inhabitants of Mesopotamia, Judea and Cappadocia. . . ." (vv. 9-11). Luke's insistence on the number and variety of the nations that witness the prodigy of Pentecost through their representatives makes it quite likely that he sees a symbolic significance here. In and through his Jewish audience Peter is already evangelizing, in some sense, all the nations of the earth.

The conclusion of Peter's speech may be compared with the conclusion of Jesus' sermon at Nazareth, and also with the conclusion of Paul's speeches at Antioch in Pisidia and at Rome. Peter declares: "The promise is for you and for your children, and for all who are far off, as many as the Lord will call" (v. 39). The last words in this statement are inspired by Joel 3:5, the beginning of which verse Peter has already cited earlier in his speech (v. 21). The complete verse from Joel runs this way: "And then whoever will call on the name of the Lord will be saved, for on Mount Zion and in Jerusalem will be those who are saved, as the Lord has said, and those to whom glad tidings are announced, whom the Lord will call." For Joel's expression, "those who are on Mount Zion and in

Jerusalem," Peter substitutes a more specific expression, "you and your children, and all those who are far off." Clearly the horizon has shifted somewhat, and Peter's change of perspective is accompanied by the use of an expression in which we may recognize the influence of Isaiah 57:19, a promise of peace "for those who are far off and for those who are near."

The Letter to the Ephesians quotes this same text from Isaiah and gives us an interpretation of it, identifying "those who are far off" with the Gentiles and "those who are near" with the Jews (Ephesians 2:13). Within Acts itself there is probably another allusion to this text of Isaiah and its Christian interpretation in a passage in which Paul related a vision granted to him in the temple, in which the Lord ordered him to leave Jerusalem and gave as his reason: "For I will send you to the nations *far away*" (22:21). The expression "all those who are *far off*" (2:39), which forms an antithesis to the phrase "to you and your children," applies rather naturally, therefore, to the Gentiles, or, more precisely, to the many among the Gentiles "who will be called by the Lord."

Confirmation for this interpretation may be found by comparing this ending of Peter's first speech with the ending of his second speech:

> You are the sons of the prophets and of the covenant that God struck with our fathers when he told Abraham, "In your descendants all the nations of the earth will be blessed." It is first of all for your sake that God raised up his servant and sent him to bless you (3:25-26).

The promise made to Abraham will be realized by the risen Christ, and Peter specifies that it will be realized "for you *first*." This seems to imply that it will be realized for others at a later stage, and the context clearly spells out the details: "In your descendants [Israel] all the nations of the earth will be blessed." The blessing is for Israel first, and then for all the nations of the earth. Still further confirmation can be found in another passage of Acts, in which the same adverb reappears: "It was necessary that the word of God be announced to you *first*. Since you reject it ... we turn to the Gentiles [to the nations]" (13:46-47).

Thus both of Peter's early speeches to the Jews end with a widening of the horizon and an intimation of the coming evangelization of the Gentiles. The details we have been emphasizing may not yet yield a complete picture of Luke's intentions; they are only clues and pointers, the exact bearing of which only the remainder of the narrative may make perfectly clear. Yet Christian readers can grasp these hints. It is significant that Luke has inserted these pointers at the end of the first two great speeches in Acts. The similarity with the conclusion of the inaugural discourses of Jesus and Paul indicates that Luke is composing these speeches purposely. We discover a genuine consistency in Luke's thinking which enables him to grasp and express a profound unity in the various stages of the salvation history he is writing.

St. Peter and Cornelius, the Centurion of Caesarea

We have already spoken of Jesus' opening sermon and his last words, and of Paul's first speech and his final declaration. Since we have just been considering Peter's inaugural discourse, the obvious thing at this point would seem to be an analysis of Peter's closing statements in the Book of Acts. The last words Peter speaks to us are at the Council of Jerusalem, at which he opts for one of two opposed positions in the debate about admission of the uncircumcised into the Church (15:7-11). But as a matter of fact Peter's contribution to that debate comes down essentially to this: that he reiterates and highlights the lesson to be drawn from the story of the conversion of the centurion Cornelius.

Luke attributes considerable importance to this incident in the arrangement of his book. He not only treats this episode at seemingly disproportionate length, but he deliberately stages events in such a way that in his story Cornelius becomes the first Gentile received into the Christian community. Just as Paul's arrival in Rome and his preaching to the pagans of the imperial city constitute the culmination of his apostolic career, we may say that, in Luke's vision, the baptism of Cornelius constitutes the culmination of Peter's apostolic career, his decisive contribution to Luke's history, after which he has only to fade away, yielding the spotlight to Paul.

In addressing the Council of Jerusalem, Peter makes of Cornelius' baptism an exemplary case:

> From the first days God chose me from among you so that the Gentiles might hear from my mouth the word of the Good News and embrace the faith (15:7).

Peter was the very first to announce the Gospel to the Gentiles, and not to a single individual merely but to the Gentiles in general. This he did in accordance with God's own plan, for God had clearly revealed his will in this regard by repeating the Pentecost miracle for the Gentiles:

> And God who knows hearts has borne witness on behalf of the Gentiles by giving them the Holy Spirit, just as he did to us (v. 8).

God has abolished every difference between Jew and Gentile, desiring to save both of them by his grace alone (v. 11).

Peter finishes speaking, and the importance of his proclamation is emphasized by the silence which ensues in the hitherto divided assembly. Barnabas and Paul then offer their testimony (v. 12), and to this James adds the testimony of the prophets (vv. 14-18). Thus the experience of the centurion from Caesarea supplies a precedent and provides the basis for a solution that ratifies in a definitive way the apostolic activity of Paul. In the order of events within Acts the honor of having opened the gates of the Church to the Gentiles belongs to Peter. Once those gates are opened, Paul will be able to do the rest.

The importance that Luke attributes to the conversion of Cornelius is proportionate to the influence of that event on the decision reached in Jerusalem. The narrative which tells of Cornelius' conversion is far from homogeneous in itself; in fact it is possible to detect in it two quite distinct centers of interest. First there is the question of the relations between Jews and Gentiles. This is underlined by Peter's remarks on entering the home of Cornelius: "You know that it is absolutely forbidden for a Jew to associate with a foreigner or to enter his house" (10:28). And for his behavior in this matter Peter draws the reproaches of the Christians in Jerusalem: "Why did you enter the home of the uncircumcised and eat with them?" (11:3). Put in these terms, the problem concerns the rules of purity that a Jew is required to observe. Peter explains his own attitude in his statement to Cornelius: "God has shown me that no man should be called defiled or impure" (10:28). Peter is alluding at this point to his vision of the great sheet let down from heaven, and to the subsequent mandate not to call impure or defiled that which God has cleansed (10:11-16). Peter will defend himself on his return to Jerusalem by relating this vision again (11:5-10), and he will recall the vision one further time at the Council (15:9).

Alongside the problem of purity that relations with the uncircumcised create for a Jew, there is also the problem of the admission of the Gentiles into the Church. This is the point Luke emphasizes in his editorial remarks at the beginning and end of the episode describing Peter's return to Jerusalem, which constitutes an epilogue to the Cornelius story:

> Now the apostles and the brethren of Judea heard that the Gentiles too had received the word of God (11:1).

> They glorified God, saying, "Therefore to the Gentiles also God has granted repentance that leads to life!" (11:18).

Peter expresses the same viewpoint earlier in the story when he asks, "Can we refuse baptism to those who have received the Holy Spirit just as we have?" (10:47). And the same problem, the question of the admission of Gentiles into the Church, dominates the debates at the Council as well (cf. 15:1, 5, 7, 14, 16f.).

Of these two centers of interest which emerge in the narrative of Cornelius' conversion, Luke is especially interested in the second. The centurion's story occupies such an important position in Acts because it is related to a larger issue. The conversion of Cornelius is not a merely individual case, for in the light of this one case Jerusalem will come to recognize the principle of the accession of the Gentiles as such into the Church.

The importance of this event is emphasized in a great missionary discourse, in which the significance of the incident is also explained (10:34-43). From the outset of the speech Peter observes:

I notice truly that God is no respecter of persons, but that *in every nation* he who fears him and practices justice is agreeable to him (vv. 34-35).

Hence it is not necessary to belong to the people of Israel in order to be pleasing to God, since Jesus is "the Lord of *all*" (v. 36). And Peter ends with the observation:

To him all the prophets bear witness to this effect, that *everyone* who believes in him will receive, through his name, remission of his sins (v. 43).

Whether Jew or Greek, one must believe in Christ in order to be saved. Thus Peter already expresses with perfect clarity in this earlier speech the position that will carry the day at the Council of Jerusalem (15:9, 11).

The Caesarea episode stands out so sharply in Acts because of the significance of the event itself. It provides solemn sanction for the principle of the accession of the Gentiles to salvation. It is the step by which Christianity passes beyond the limits of Judaism. It will be necessary, subsequently, to gather sufficient momentum for expansion "to the ends of the earth," as will happen in fact in the ministry of Paul. But as of this moment the first decisive step has already been taken, and Peter, his role now finished, makes his final exit from the stage.

III. THE APOSTLE TO THE GENTILES

Peter gave events a wise and decisive turn. It is now up to Paul to spread the message of salvation to the ends of the earth, to announce it to the Gentiles all the way to the capital of the pagan world. After the Council of Jerusalem (Acts 15) Paul will be the only main actor in the story, and even prior to that point he has an important role to play. Paul is undoubtedly the principal figure in the Acts of the Apostles. In this book of slightly more than 1,000 verses, he occupies the foreground in about 600, Peter in only 250. But it is not merely a matter of quantity. Paul is the personality of whom Acts gives us the most complete and lifelike picture. Starting with his role in the martyrdom of Stephen and continuing up to the period of his stay in Rome, his whole life is known to us, or at least Luke wishes to convey that impression. We have already noted the triple mention of his journey to Rome, which echoes the triple mention of Jesus' journey to Jerusalem in the central section of Luke's Gospel. But there is no need to belabor the obvious. Paul's position in Acts is so crucial that we may assert without fear of exaggerating that, if we can grasp the significance Luke sees in Paul's mission, we will have understood by the same token the meaning Luke intends to convey by his entire narrative.

How then does Luke conceive Paul's mission? It will be easy to discover the answer to this question by looking at a few select passages in Acts. We will consider first some texts which explicitly define the purpose and scope of Paul's activity; one such statement is given by Paul himself at the end of his final speech, and other such definitions are found in earlier narratives which describe Paul's call to the apostolate. After that we will consider the episode in Athens, which Luke has made the symbolic climax in his presentation of Paul's mission.

The Scope of Paul's Mission

1. Luke does not represent Paul's preaching in Rome by any fully developed speech; he merely indicates Paul's theme and quotes his concluding declaration. But elsewhere in Acts we do find attributed to Paul speeches worthy of the name. There is the address in the synagogue at Antioch in Pisidia, representative of his preaching before the Jews; the one in Athens, typical of his preaching before pagan audiences; the speech in Miletus, the pastoral will and testament of the apostle, addressed to those who will have to take over the care of the churches he founded. Finally there are the three apologias before the people of Jerusalem, before Felix, and before King Agrippa respectively. For the last of these occasions, the rather solemn appearance before Agrippa, Luke supplies a long and very elaborate discourse (26:2-23).

At the end of this speech Paul formulates a definition of his own preaching. He tells us that his purpose in preaching is to demonstrate, with the help of Scripture, three points:

(1) that it was necessary that the Christ should suffer and that (2) having risen from the dead (3) he should announce the light to the people [Israel] and to the [pagan] nations (26:23).

Let us turn back now to the final words of Jesus to his apostles, where we read:

Thus it was written (1) that the Christ should suffer (2) and that he would rise on the third day (3) and that in his name repentance for the remission of sins should be proclaimed to all the (pagan) nations, beginning from Jerusalem (Luke 24:46-47).

The parallelism between the two passages is striking. The purpose of Paul's preaching, like that of Jesus' teaching, is to reveal the "messianic signs" contained in Scripture and fulfilled in Jesus: suffering, resurrection, salvation carried to all nations. The first two signs are realized in Jesus' death and resurrection. The third sign is fulfilled in the mission of Paul. Through him the work of Christ is carried on to the end, and the history of salvation is brought to completion.

2. On the road to Damascus, Saul the persecutor was transformed into an apostle of Christ—a decisive event whose import is incalculable for the destiny of the Church. And to stress its significance Luke employs a familiar device. Just as he reveals his interest in Cornelius' conversion by relating each of its episodes twice, so he shows us the importance he attributes to Paul's conversion by giving us no less than three detailed reports of the theophany on the Damascus road (9:1-19; 22:5-16; 26:12-18).

Each of these accounts underscores the universal character of the mission entrusted to Paul. In the first, Jesus tells the aged Ananias: "This man is for me a chosen instrument to carry my name before [pagan] nations, kings, and the children of Israel" (9:15). In the second, Ananias tells Paul: "You must be a witness before all men to what you have seen and heard" (22:15). The expression "all men" is vague, but chosen on purpose here, for when later Paul explicitly states that the Lord has sent him to the Gentiles (v. 21), the outcries of his listeners will prevent him from continuing his speech. In the third narrative, Jesus declares directly to Paul, with allusions to the prophecies of Jeremiah 1:5-8 and Isaiah 42:7, 16: "I am sending you to the [pagan] nations to open their eyes, so that they may turn from darkness to light, and from the dominion of Satan to God. ..." (26:17-18).

This manner of defining Paul's mission as specially concerned with the Gentiles corresponds to what Paul writes about it himself in his Letter to the Galatians: "It pleased God to reveal his Son to me, so that I might bring this Good News to the Gentiles" (1:16). Hence the meaning Luke sees in the Damascus event is no different from the meaning it had for Paul himself. Luke is quite aware of the specific mission entrusted to Paul, and the position he assigns Paul in Acts is directly related to the intention behind the book as a whole. It is precisely as the apostle of the Gentiles that Paul receives the starring role in Acts, as the instrument chosen by God to carry the message of salvation to the pagan nations.

Paul in Athens

Athens, located midway between Jerusalem and Rome, stands at the center of the history of Paul's mission and receives special treatment from Luke. If we can judge from what Paul tells us of his mood in the aftermath of his visit to Athens (1 Corinthians 1:17—2:5, esp. 2:3), we may imagine that he did not have a very happy memory of his visit there, but seems to have carried away only a feeling of painful failure. Furthermore, he stayed only a very short time in Athens, whereas we see him afterward settling down in Corinth for almost two years and founding there one of his main churches. Yet Luke, who scarcely mentions the Galatians, and allots only nine verses to Thessalonica and eighteen to Corinth, devotes fully twenty verses to Athens and localizes there one of Paul's most brilliant speeches. Cultivated man that he was, Luke appears to have been sensitive to the prestige of Athens. Athens in New Testament times no longer had any political importance. It was essentially a university town, but the nerve center of pagan thought, the intellectual and religious center of the Graeco-Roman world. For this reason it had symbolic value. The message of salvation, destined for all men, must be heard in this lofty forum. At an earlier point in his story, during Paul's sojourn in Lystra, Luke had already drawn a rapid preliminary sketch of Paul's preaching before pagan audiences, but he was waiting for a more solemn occasion on which to provide a more complete example of it. Athens offered him that occasion.

Paul speaks first of all before philosophers, representatives of the main schools then in fashion. Next he appears before the Areopagus, which occupied, in Luke's estimation, approximately the same position in Athens that the Sanhedrin did in Jerusalem: it was the high court empowered to judge in doctrinal matters. In Paul's time the Areopagus no longer held its meetings on the hill from which its name derived, but beneath the royal portico, at the very spot where Socrates had been accused of introducing new gods into the city. Luke discreetly suggests the parallel: the philosophers bring Paul before the Areopagus and request an explanation from him because they recognize him as a "preacher of foreign gods" (17:18).

Paul cleverly alludes to the "unknown god" to whom the Athenians have raised an altar, and, taking that as his starting point, goes on to announce to them the one true God. His argumentation is rhetorically brilliant, but the underlying themes he develops are commonplaces of the monotheistic propaganda current in Hellenistic Judaism. These themes include:

A. criticism of pagan temples: "The God who made the world and all that is in it, he, the Lord of heaven and earth, does not dwell in temples made by human hands" (v. 24).

B. criticism of the worship paid in those temples: "Neither is he served by human hands, as if he were in need of anything" (v. 25).

C. criticism of the idols, that is, the statues that are honored in the temples: "We should not think that the divinity is like gold or silver or stone graven by human art and ingenuity" (v. 29).

Then comes Paul's conclusion, which touches our subject more directly. After the Judaeo-Hellenistic tone of the body of the speech, the conclusion sounds a specifically Christian note:

> God has overlooked the times of ignorance, but he now makes known to all men everywhere that they must repent, because he has set a day on which to judge the universe with justice by a man whom he has appointed, and he has given all a guarantee of that by raising that man from the dead (vv. 30-31).

The message is addressed "to all men everywhere," an expression which is a more literary variation of the formula "to all the nations" (Luke 24:27), or "to the ends of the earth" (Acts 1:8). Furthermore, as Bornkamm has already noticed, the final detail of the discourse recalls its beginning:

> From a unique principle God made *the whole human race*, so that it might dwell over *the whole face of the earth* (v. 26).

At the beginning there was a single man, and from him the whole human race spread over the whole face of the earth; and at the end of time, all men everywhere will be judged by one man, the one whom God raised from the dead. Luke's language suggests a parallelism between the two Adams and emphasizes in a new way the universal character of the economy of salvation inaugurated by Jesus' resurrection. The Easter event, an anticipatory sign of the final judgment, has the same universal dimensions as the creation of Adam, the father of the entire human race.

The assertion that the message of salvation must be carried to all the nations is generally based on the prophecies of the latter half of the Book of Isaiah (40:5; 42:7, 16; 49:6; 57:19). The speech at Nazareth raises an argument based on the example of the prophets Elijah and Elisha. The speech at Athens appeals to a wider consideration, but one that is also based on the Bible: the universal role which falls to the Christ at the judgment corresponds, in its extension, to the role of the first man, the origin of all humanity. The practical point of the argumentation in these various speeches is always the same, namely that the message of salvation is to be announced to all men and all nations.

IV. CONCLUSION

All the investigations we have conducted into Luke's text, at its most significant points, yield one identical result. We have discovered that in writing the Book of Acts Luke wished to show how the message of salvation, the Gospel of Jesus Christ, was revealed to "all flesh," how it reached "the ends of the earth," and how God's favors came to be bestowed upon "foreigners"—in a word, how the apostolic preaching turned toward the pagan world.

The viewpoint Luke adopts in narrating the expansion of the Gospel message is not that of a chronicler. He is not content merely to relate the circumstances that led to the spread of the Church among the pagans. He wishes to show that this new orientation was willed by God and guided by the Holy Spirit, and thus that it fulfilled the messianic prophecies. Therefore the story Luke tells has a theological meaning, and Luke is at pains to highlight that aspect of the story. The history Luke records contributes a specific and irreplaceable element to the demonstration that Jesus is the Messiah promised by the prophets, for the promised Messiah was not merely to undergo death and rise from the dead but was also to assure that the Good News of salvation would be proclaimed, in his own name, to all the nations.

We have discovered the theological concern on Luke's part which induced him to follow up his Gospel by writing the Book of Acts. The correspondence between Old Testament prophecy and early Christian history, as between prediction and fulfillment, supposes a process that we may look at from either end. Thus if it is true that the evangelization of the Gentiles fulfills messianic prophecies, it is equally true to say that the messianic prophecies guarantee the legitimacy of such evangelization. They present it as part of the program set down by God for the Messiah. The viewpoint Luke wishes to express in Acts is complex. He wishes to teach us that the Scriptures have in fact been fulfilled. He also wants us to understand that the Scriptures themselves justify the Christian mission among the pagans, for they require this mission as the continuation of the salvific work of Jesus, the Christ.

The First Christian Pentecost

Our Christian feast of Pentecost builds upon an earlier Jewish feast commemorating the promulgation of the Law on Sinai. Though that Jewish feast was eventually displaced and surpassed by the Christian celebration of Pentecost, its contribution to our Christian Pentecost was enormous. We are indebted to it for the wealth of biblical associations and religious reflection that have carried over into our own liturgy and that give Pentecost the deeper theological significance it possesses for us in the Church today.

The way that the author of the Acts of the Apostles tells the Pentecost story reveals his intention to clarify this mysterious event by means of Old Testament Scriptures. The use he makes of Joel 3:1-5 in Acts 2:17-21, 33, 39 is especially revealing in this respect. Equally significant is the allusion in Acts 2:33 to Psalm 68:19, a psalm which the synagogue applied to the bestowal of the Law but which the early Church applies to the bestowal of the Spirit (cf. Ephesians 4:8-11). Although the Pentecost story in Acts has passed through a process of very personal editing at Luke's hands, the memory of the theophany on Mount Sinai and traces of Jewish traditions connected with that theophany can still be detected in the narrative that Luke has given to us.

We wish to discover some of these allusions and overtones in the account of Pentecost. We desire also to enter into Luke's own point of view in telling the story, for a sacred author is always concerned to communicate, along with the facts he narrates, his personal interpretation and evaluation of those facts. To grasp that personal viewpoint, we must first of all understand the text as he composed it. Though the text is not an easy one and raises a number of difficulties for interpreters, we will attempt to state simply and clearly the interpretations that seem most convincing to us.

35

I. THE COMING OF THE SPIRIT

When the day of Pentecost arrived, they were all together in the same place, when suddenly there came from heaven a loud noise like a violent windstorm, which filled the whole house where they were. There appeared to them tongues as of fire; they divided, and one came to rest on each of them. They were all filled with the Holy Spirit and began to speak in other tongues, as the Spirit gave them the power to speak (Acts 2:1-4).

The Day of Pentecost

A. The date on which the event takes place is *Pentecost*, the Greek name for the feast celebrated on the "fiftieth" day after Passover. In Hebrew its traditional name was "feast of Weeks," because of the requirement to "count seven complete weeks, beginning with the day after the sabbath, the day on which you bring the sheaf of the wave-offering" (Leviticus 23:15). Since this required method of computation was not entirely clear, however, we discover in the first century three different ways of calculating the fifty days. The Sadducees start counting from the feast of Passover, the Pharisees from the sabbath after Passover, and the Essenes from the sabbath following the Passover octave. The Essene system of computation had the advantage of making Pentecost coincide with the date that Exodus 19:1 assigns to the events on Sinai: "Three months after the children of Israel had come out of Egypt, on that very day. . . ." However, the Pharisees also managed to get both of these dates to coincide, simply by reading "on the sixth day" instead of "on the same day."

B. The chronological notations in Acts are no clearer than those in the Pentateuch. Luke writes literally: "As the day of Pentecost *was being fulfilled.*" At first sight this would seem to mean, "As the day of Pentecost was coming to an end," but that meaning is definitely excluded by verse 15, where we are told that it is only nine o'clock in the morning. Furthermore, we do find similar expressions elsewhere, and they show that the construction employed here is elliptical. For example, Luke writes in his Gospel: "For Elizabeth the time of her delivery was fulfilled" (1:57). Clearly this does not mean that the child's birth had already taken place, but that the time for it had come; what is completed or fulfilled is the time leading up to the birth. Similarly Luke speaks in Acts 2:1 of the fulfillment of the period that leads up to Pentecost, and since that period has come to an end we must conclude that the day of the feast itself has come. The ancient translations and the Vulgate substituted the plural for the singular, reading, "As the days of Pentecost were being fulfilled." This change makes the text more intelligible, and we believe it renders its real meaning quite well.

Exegetes would agree in general with this interpretation. Some would give more weight, however, to Luke's use of a present tense in this expression, where an aorist or a perfect might more naturally be expected, and thus would urge that the present here has the force of a future tense: the day of Pentecost was about to be fulfilled; it was near but not yet there. But in our opinion it is unlikely that the present tense carries such a future nuance in this verse. More probably Luke's intention was to stress the coincidence of the event with the Jewish feast which serves as its background and permits us to grasp its deeper meaning. A few other authors attribute a theological value to the verb Luke uses, as if he were thinking of the "fulfillment" of divine promises or the divine plan, and would therefore translate: "As the promised day had come, the day of Pentecost." But this interpretation seems to read more meaning into the verb than it can contain or than the parallels suggest.

C. "They were *all* together in the same place." It is not easy to determine exactly who is included in the group mentioned here. Some believe that Luke is referring to all the one hundred and twenty persons mentioned in 1:15. Others are of the opinion that the word "all" here applies only to the apostles and the additional persons mentioned in 1:14: "a few women, including Mary, the mother of Jesus, and his brothers."

The second of these explanations seems more probable to us. Notice first of all the strong connection which the editor establishes between 2:1-2 and 1:13-14. The expression "they were all together in the same place" (2:1) echoes "all these were applying themselves together...." (1:14). And the phrase "the house in which they were" (2:2) echoes "the upper room in which they were staying" (1:13). We should also notice that 2:7 describes all the recipients of the outpouring of the Spirit as Galileans, and yet it would be rash to presume that the one hundred and twenty persons mentioned in 1:15 were all from Galilee.

Furthermore, when Peter starts speaking, Luke mentions only the eleven at his side (v. 14). It is important, too, to recall how insistently Luke has announced the Pentecost event ahead of time and how he has reiterated the promise that is to be fulfilled when Pentecost comes (Luke 24:49; Acts 1:4-5, 8). But this promise is addressed only to the apostles, and it would be strange indeed to find a much larger group sharing in its realization.

As a matter of fact, the list of persons mentioned in 1:13-14 constituted the original and normal introduction to the Pentecost narrative, but it became separated from that narrative in the present text because Luke desired to describe how the twelfth apostle came to be elected. The episode of the choice of Matthias is only parenthetical, and the mention of the hundred and twenty persons in 1:15 is a second parenthetical remark within the first. At the conclusion of the election-narrative Luke is careful to call our attention back to the essential point of the story: "The lot fell to Matthias, who was added to the eleven apostles. When the day of Pentecost arrived, they were all together in the same place. . . ." (1:26—2:1). The "all" in 2:1, then, clearly includes the apostles, and most probably also includes the few other persons whose presence has already been mentioned in 1:14.

D. The expression "all *together* in the same place" refers directly to an external togetherness in space; yet if we take into account Luke's vocabulary and the corresponding passage in 1:13-14, occupying the same space together seems to suppose and express another kind of closeness as well: unanimity, union of hearts. Similarly, when the Law was promulgated on Sinai, "all the people responded *together*" (the adverb here is *yahdaw* in Hebrew; the Greek translation is *homothymadon*, "unanimously"), committing themselves to carry out God's orders (Exodus 19:8). Jewish tradition stressed the theme of unanimity in this context. The Targum introduces that note at the very beginning of the story: "Israel pitched camp with one heart [as one] facing the mountain" (Exodus 19:2). The Tannaite commentary explains that "the Israelites were 'of one heart' on reaching Mount Sinai, and they were 'of one heart' when responding to Moses," and returns to the same theme a little later: "When they were all at Mount Sinai to receive the Law, they were all 'of one heart' to accept with joy the kingdom of God" (Mekhiltha Exodus 19:2, 8; 20:2). The unanimity of the Christian community at the time of Pentecost corresponds to the unanimity of the assembly of Israel at the foot of Mount Sinai.

The Loud Noise

A. The coming of the Spirit is accompanied by two perceptible phenomena, the first of which is described as a *resounding noise.*   2: 2 The Greek word which Luke uses at this point is *echos*, which is applied elsewhere to the roar of the sea (Luke 21:25; cf. Psalm 65:7), to thunder (Sirach 46:17), or to the shrill sound of a trumpet (Exodus 19:16; Hebrews 12:19; Psalm 150:3). In verse 6 below, Luke will designate the same phenomenon by the word *phone*, which, as used there, merely denotes a "sound" without specifying that it is very loud.

Outside of Acts 2:2, the word *echos* is employed in the New Testament only by the author of the Epistle to the Hebrews, who draws a contrast between Christian experience and the experience of the Israelites at Sinai: "It was no sensible external reality *you* came in touch with," he reminds his fellow Christians, "no burning fire, darkness, gloom, tempest, trumpet-blast (*echoi*) or sound (*phonei*) of words. . . ." (Hebrews 12:18-19). Unlike the Israelites, to whom God manifested himself in that perceptible way on Mount Sinai, Christians have been able to approach God quietly and without uproar, through faith, on Mount Zion, the heavenly Jerusalem (v. 22).

The Sinai theophany is recalled here especially in the terms in which it is described in Exodus: "And it happened, the third day, when morning came, that there were sounds (*phonai*: peals of thunder) and lightning-flashes and a dark cloud over Mount Sinai; the voice (*phone*) of a trumpet resounded (*echei*) loudly" (19:16). Philo, in his treatise on *The Decalogue*, develops this material from Exodus in greater detail. He pictures God creating in the air an invisible noise (*echon*), which transforms the air into a flaming fire (#33). He speaks in a later passage of a sound (*phone*) which resounded (*exechei*) from the midst of the fire that spread out from the sky (*ap'ouranou*); the flames changed into a language (*eis dialekton*) adapted to the hearers, and its words were pronounced with such clarity that they gave the impression of being seen rather than heard (#46; cf. Exodus 20:18).

These speculations reveal the close attention which first-century Judaism paid to details of the narrative of the theophany on Sinai. It is quite easy for us to believe, therefore, that Luke's description of Pentecost in Acts would have reminded Jewish readers of that spectacular scene on Sinai. By alluding in his Pentecost episode to several very well known features of that scene, such as the "resounding noise" which is also a "sound," Luke establishes a parallelism between the two events. In this way he subtly suggests that the first Christian Pentecost is a repetition of the original theophany on Sinai which was commemorated by the Jewish feast of Pentecost.

B. The resounding noise comes *from heaven*, like the voice heard at the baptism of Jesus (Luke 3:22 par.), or by Peter in Joppa (Acts 11:9), and by the seer of the Book of Revelation (10:4 and *passim*). It also resembles the resounding voice on Sinai: "[God] made his voice heard from heaven" (Deuteronomy 4:36; cf. Exodus 19:3b; 20:22).

C. Luke also emphasizes the *suddenness* of the sound. The adverb here translated "suddenly" (*aphno*) is a Lucan word, for we meet it again in the New Testament only in Acts 16:26 and 28:6. To Luke we should also attribute the comparison of the noise to *a violent windstorm*, which reminds us of the description of the shipwreck in Acts 27:40-41. Luke does not say that there was any real wind at Pentecost, but that the sound which manifested the presence of the Spirit resembled the sound of a strong driving wind. In Greek, the terms for "wind" (*pnoe*) and for "Spirit" (*pneuma*) are closely related (cf. John 3:8).

D. Finally, this noise *filled the whole house* where they were gathered. As we have already mentioned, this house can only be the one which contained "the upper room where the apostles were staying" (1:13). The noise "filled" the whole house, just as the Holy Spirit will be said to "fill" all those who were in it (v. 4). This remark might naturally remind us of another detail from the Sinai theophany: "Mount Sinai was entirely (*holon*) wrapped in smoke, for the Lord had come down upon it in the fire" (Exodus 19:18).

The Tongues of Fire

A. After the audial phenomenon comes a visual one: "tongues appeared," or more literally: "tongues *were seen* by them" (v. 3). This expression is typically Lucan. When Matthew wants to describe a vision, he tends to write that "an angel appeared (*ephane*)" to someone, for example to Joseph (Matthew 1:20; 2:13, 19). Luke, however, always says that "an angel was seen (*ophthesan*)" by someone (Luke 1:11; 22:43; Acts 7:30, 35). For example, God "was seen" by Abraham (Acts 7:2), and the risen Jesus "was seen" by Peter or Paul (Luke 24:34; Acts 9:17; 26:16; cf. 1 Corinthians 15:5-8). These are all instances of supernatural appearances in which the person "seen" makes himself visible or is rendered visible by God. Therefore the apostles at Pentecost were also witnesses to the revelation of a supernatural reality.

B. The object seen here looks like *tongues* of fire. The Greek word for "tongue" (*glossa*), like the Hebrew *lashon*, designates not only the organ we use in speaking or the language we speak; it can also apply to any object that has the shape of a tongue, in the sense in which we can speak in English of the tongue of a shoe or a bell. One obvious motive for Luke's choice of the word "tongue" at this point is that he wants to indicate a relation between the vision that is seen and the gift of "tongues" that is granted to the apostles (v. 4).

Yet we must admit that "tongues of *fire*" is not an entirely natural expression. We might occasionally speak of fire "licking" something it is about to consume (Isaiah 5:24 contains a similar image), but it would be more natural for us, and for Luke, to speak simply of a "flame" rather than a "tongue of fire." As a matter of fact it is precisely flames that the apostles at Pentecost do see. Yet Luke may have had a further motive for his use of the expression "tongues of *fire*," for it is another reminder of the Sinai theophany, in which fire also played an important role (Exodus 19:18; Deuteronomy 4:5). Luke is careful to point out, however, that the tongues were not really fire but merely looked like it; it is typical of Luke to make clear in this way that he is speaking of a mere appearance (cf. also Luke 3:22).

C. When the apostles perceive them, the fire-like tongues are *dividing* (the tense of the participle is present). This verb is Lucan in a special sense, for we find it in the other Gospels only in the citation: "They have divided my garments among them" (Psalm 22:19; Luke 23:34 and par.), but we find it a number of times in Luke's special material. His use of the verb at this point suggests another connection with the rabbinic traditions concerning the events on Sinai, for on that holy mountain God's voice was supposed to have "divided" into seven voices, and then again into seventy voices or tongues, as many tongues as there were peoples. The following saying, for instance, is attributed to R. Johanan (mid-third century A.D.): "The [divine] voice issued forth and *divided* into seventy voices, into seventy tongues, so that all peoples might hear it; and each people heard the voice in its own tongue." We cannot be certain that such traditions existed as early as the first century, yet we have no right to ignore such parallels. At the very least they suggest that the idea of a "dividing" of God's voice or word during the process of its communication to men is quite in line with a Jewish reading of the biblical narrative of the promulgation of the Law.

D. "And one came to rest on each of them." The Greek text is less clear than this, for it simply says, "and came to rest on each of them," leaving the subject of the verb unexpressed. However, it is easy enough to supply a subject from the "tongues" that have just been described as dividing; now one tongue comes to rest on each of those present. Alternatively, Luke may use the singular verb here because he is thinking less of the "tongues" themselves than he is of the Holy Spirit who is manifested by these tongues, and who will be mentioned in the phrase immediately following: " And all were filled with the Holy Spirit" (v. 4).

"It came to rest" is an imperfect translation of the Greek verb *ekathisen*, which means more precisely, "it established itself." In connection with the baptism of Jesus, the Synoptics say that the Spirit "came down" upon him (Luke 3:22 and par.), but John specifies that the Spirit "came down and remained" upon him (1:32-33). The verb Luke employs here in Acts 2:3 has a similar nuance; it connotes a "taking over." The Spirit, who comes upon the disciples in the form of tongues, "settles upon them."

Filled with the Holy Spirit

Luke, who has been carefully building his composition to a climax, has already mentioned a resounding noise, like a strong squall, and the appearance of fire-like tongues—both signs that announce a divine presence—but up to this point he has not mentioned the Spirit. Finally now in verse 4 he mentions him twice by name, the Spirit of God, who is recognized the moment he takes possession of a soul.

A. Of "all" those present (cf. v. 1), Luke writes that they were "*filled* with the Holy Spirit." Similarly Jesus had been filled with the Holy Spirit after his baptism (Luke 4:1), as had John the Baptist from his mother's womb (1:15), and as Elizabeth and Zachariah were when they were about to utter their inspired words (1:41, 67). In Acts we shall see Peter "filled" with the same Spirit (4:8), as well as Paul (9:17; 13:9), Stephen (6:5; 7:55), Barnabas (11:24), the apostles as a group (4:31), and the disciples at Antioch in Pisidia (13:52). At the starting point of the history of the Church, as at the starting point of Jesus' history, the Spirit of God is at work. And his active presence is so intense that it reveals itself in the same way as water does, for we notice that water has filled a vase only when it starts overflowing. Peter will speak on Pentecost of a "pouring out" of the Spirit (v. 7), and of Jesus, ascended into heaven, receiving the Spirit from the Father and "pouring it out" on the disciples (v. 33).

B. Since the narrative will spend some time developing the perceptible effect of the Spirit's presence, it may be useful to stress at this point the fact that the cause is more important than that effect. The Pentecost event had been predicted by Jesus, in words which Luke uses as the conclusion of his Gospel and repeats in slightly different form at the beginning of Acts:

> I will send upon you what the Father has promised. But wait here in the city, until you are clothed with the *power* from on high (Luke 24:49).

> You shall receive a *power*, that of the Holy Spirit, who will come down upon you. Then you will be my witnesses. . . . (Acts 1:8).

The image of a divine power (*dynamis*) descending upon the apostles as if to envelop them is slightly different from the image of an inner effusion which fills them to overflowing, but both images point to the same reality. The charism that attests to the Spirit's presence in the apostles is at the same time a manifestation of the supernatural power with which the Spirit clothes them.

C. The coming of the Spirit at Pentecost is announced beforehand by still another image: "John baptized with water, but you will be baptized in the Holy Spirit not many days hence" (Acts 1:5). This promise of Jesus, which is recalled once more in Acts 11:16, echoes the earlier declaration of John the Baptist:

> I baptize you with water, but One more powerful than I is coming, whose sandal-straps I am not worthy to untie, and he will baptize you in the Holy Spirit and fire (Luke 3:16).

The outpouring of the Spirit on Pentecost morning is a *baptism.* That suggests, according to the etymology of the word, that the apostles have been "immersed" or "plunged" into the Holy Spirit. In this image the Spirit is no longer compared with water that "fills" but with water that "submerges."

Once the Holy Spirit has descended from heaven upon the apostles on Pentecost morning, he will remain present henceforward in the Church, and his presence will be the characteristic mark of the Christian economy. Paul can say to every Christian:

> God has sent into our hearts the Spirit of his Son (Galatians 4:6).

> God has established us together in Christ, anointed us, stamped us with his seal, and put the Spirit into our hearts as a pledge (2 Corinthians 1:21-22).

Israel had received the Law, which taught it what conduct would be pleasing to God. But the Law was powerless to transform men, and instead of bringing them justice and life, it became the instrument of their condemnation and death. The New Covenant replaces the prescriptions of the Law by the gift of the Spirit, who really transforms hearts. The Spirit does not impose a way of life upon us from without, but inspires us from deep within ourselves to the manner of life which God desires of us. Therefore Paul can tell

Christians: "If you allow yourselves to be led by the Spirit, you are not under the Law" (Galatians 5:18). This concept of the Christian condition as an economy of the Spirit, in contrast to the regime of the Law, occupies a leading place in Pauline theology, especially as developed in 2 Corinthians, Galatians, and Romans. It is worth noting that this same antithesis is present, and its two elements stand out in strong contrast, in the context of Pentecost. For the commemoration of the Law, the central element in the Jewish feast of Pentecost, is displaced in the Christian feast and yields to another center: commemoration of the Spirit which has been poured out, and gratitude for that gift.

II. SPEAKING IN OTHER TONGUES

After describing the apostles being filled with the Holy Spirit, Luke goes on to say that "they began to speak in other tongues" (v. 4). This remark is obviously crucial for an understanding of the Pentecost narrative, and hence we must make an effort to understand clearly what Luke means by it.

The attempt to understand the phenomenon described in this verse has generated a number of theories and hypotheses. But beneath all the diverse explanations offered, we may discern two general tendencies, sufficient for our purposes. In the first, the discourses of the apostles under the influence of the Spirit are classified under the gift of tongues, and are considered to consist of sounds that have no meaning in any human language. In the second, it is supposed that the apostles spoke in tongues that were foreign to them, but that happened to be the tongues of the many foreign peoples represented in the crowd. Most authors do not feel compelled to make a choice between these two interpretations. Some are of the opinion that Luke simply set down side by side two interpretations of the Pentecost miracle that had come to him from divergent sources or traditions. Many others, however, believe that the narrative as it stands is quite homogeneous: the Spirit put into the mouth of the apostles ecstatic, humanly unintelligible speech, and at the same time he granted the listeners the capacity to understand them, each one in his own tongue.

Speaking in Tongues

Luke writes that the apostles started to "speak in other tongues" (*lalein heterais glossais*). If we overlook, for the time being, the adjective "other," we recognize at once in the expression "speaking in tongues" the name of a charism that appears to have been rather widespread in the primitive Church.

A. In Acts this expression is first employed in the story of Cornelius, the pagan centurion from Caesarea, whom Peter received along with his entire household into the Church.

> Peter was still speaking, when the Holy Spirit descended upon all who were listening to the word. And all the circumcised believers who had come with Peter were amazed, because the gift of the Holy Spirit had been poured out even on the Gentiles. For they heard them speaking in tongues and praising God (10:44-46).

Cornelius and his family "speak in tongues," that is, they utter ecstatic speech, for in this context there is no reason to suppose that they spoke foreign tongues. This episode at Caesarea is particularly important, because in several places Luke's narrative points to what happened at Pentecost as an analogous experience. The first of these texts is the question Peter puts to his fellow Christians in the home of Cornelius: "Can anyone refuse the water of baptism to those who have received the Holy Spirit, *just as we did*?" (10:47). Then on his return to Jerusalem Peter explains his conduct to the Christians there:

> I had hardly begun speaking when the Holy Spirit fell upon them, *just as he did upon us at the beginning.* Then I remembered how the Lord Jesus had said, "John baptized with water, but you will be baptized in the Holy Spirit." Therefore if God has granted to them *the same gift as to us*. . . . (11:15-17).

Finally, Peter takes up the same topic again when he tells the Council of Jerusalem: "God bore witness on their behalf by giving them the Holy Spirit, *just as he did to us*" (15:8). We should note, however, that the analogy pertains properly to the gift of the Spirit itself, rather than to the precise way in which the Spirit manifests his presence; the texts do not say that the charism granted to the

Gentiles at Caesarea was identical with the charism the apostles received on Pentecost.

The expression "speaking in tongues" recurs in the episode concerning the disciples of John the Baptist at Ephesus. We are told that "when Paul had laid his hand on them, the Holy Spirit came upon them, and they started to speak in tongues and to prophesy" (19:6). The intervention of the Spirit is revealed on this occasion not only by the use of incomprehensible "tongues," but also by inspired, perfectly intelligible speech, as in the gift of "prophecy."

B. St. Paul gives us more details about the gift of tongues in the long passage he devotes to that subject in the First Letter to the Corinthians (chs. 12—14). Faced with what he considers excessive infatuation with this extraordinary charism on the part of the Christians in Corinth, Paul's first concern is to stress the usefulness of the wide variety of different charisms that the Spirit bestows. The Corinthians should not be surprised that not all speak in tongues (12:30), since the Spirit gives "varieties of tongues" (*gene glosson*, vv. 10, 28) only to some Christians, while to some others he grants the gift of "interpretation of tongues" (v. 10) which complements the former. There is one gift that all should aspire to, and without which it would be of no avail even to "speak in tongues of men and of angels." That is the gift of love (ch. 13).

Paul observes, further, that "he who speaks in tongues does not speak to men, but to God, for nobody understands him, but he utters mysteries in the Spirit" (14:2). He who "speaks in a tongue" does not contribute to the building up of the community, unless there is someone present who can interpret what he says in intelligible language (vv. 4-13). Furthermore, the understanding of the person who "prays in a tongue" remains sterile, so that he does not even grasp the meaning of his own prayer (v. 14). To the observer, the gift of "speaking in tongues" resembles delirium, as in the scene Paul conjures up: "What if outsiders or unbelievers should enter your assembly and find all of you speaking in tongues? Won't they imagine that you are out of your minds?" (v. 23). In practice, therefore, when the community comes together, it will be wise to limit the exercise of tongues: let only two people, or at most three, speak in tongues at any single gathering, provided there is also an interpreter present.

C. Both Acts and 1 Corinthians mention "speaking in tongues." *Are both works referring to the same gift?* It would appear so. Certainly the expressions used by Paul and Luke (at least in Acts 10:46 and 19:6) are identical, and there are several further indications that they may be referring to an identical gift. Notice first of all that 1 Corinthians 14 admirably accounts for the mention of the two key charisms together again in Acts 19:6: "They were speaking in tongues and prophesying."

Another piece of evidence, and one that is more important for the interpretation of the Pentecost miracle, is that the "speaking in tongues" at Pentecost calls forth among some in the assembly a reaction very similar to the one Paul would expect among unbelievers who might witness a glossolalia session in the Church of Corinth. Paul comments: "Won't they imagine that you are out of your minds (*mainesthe*)?" (1 Corinthians 14:23). And Luke narrates that some in the crowd at Pentecost "said in mockery: 'They are full of new wine!' " (Acts 2:13). In other words, the apostles do give the impression of being drunk, and this expression of the crowd's opinion provides Peter with the starting point for his speech: "No, these people are not drunk, as you suppose, for it is only the third hour of the day" (v. 15). Clearly the analogy with drunkenness is more striking and appropriate if the apostles were speaking in "incoherent" tongues than if they were speaking a language in which everyone present could recognize his own mother tongue.

A third point of comparison deserves attention. Paul is of the opinion that a person who "speaks in tongues" speaks to God, prays, blesses God, and gives him thanks (1 Corinthians 14:2, 14-17, 28). The words spoken may be unintelligible to those gathered around, but God understands them and is honored by them. Luke records that those present at Caesarea were aware of the Spirit coming upon Cornelius and his household precisely because they heard them "speaking in tongues and magnifying (*megalynein*) God" (Acts 10:46), and he specifies that those present at Pentecost heard the apostles "speaking of the mighty works (*lalein ta megaleia*) of God" (2:11). These statements in Acts seem, at first sight, to correspond rather well with the sense Paul attributes to speaking in tongues in his remarks to the Corinthians. Yet, in fact, it is necessary to examine this apparent resemblance more carefully.

The expression used in connection with Cornelius, namely that he and his household were "speaking in tongues and magnifying God," might be taken in several ways. The two verbs employed might be considered to describe two aspects of a single utterance, and despite the presence of the coordinating conjunction ("and"), the sentence could be read as subordinating one idea to another; the meaning would be something like, "they spoke in tongues, magnifying God," or else, "as they spoke in tongues, they magnified God." Such a construction would not be very unusual. Yet the more natural and obvious interpretation of the expression would take the two verbs as designating two distinct kinds of utterance: the Spirit manifested his presence, on the one hand, by means of speech in tongues, and, on the other hand, by eliciting praise which everyone present could understand. The parallel passage in Acts 19:6 clearly favors this latter interpretation: the disciples of John the Baptist at Ephesus "spoke in tongues and prophesied." Elsewhere, songs addressed to God belong to the genre of "prophecy," as in the case of Zachariah who "was filled with the Holy Spirit and prophesied, saying 'Blessed be the Lord, the God of Israel' " (Luke 1:67ff.). Hence it seems preferably in Acts 10:46 as well to distinguish two manifestations of the Spirit: Cornelius and his household speak in tongues *and* extol the great works of God.

Let us come back to the Pentecost narrative. Those who gather around the apostles after the coming of the Spirit declare: "We hear them speaking in our tongues about the great works of God." The phrase "in our tongues" shows, of course, that the apostles' speech was intelligible. Though they were addressing God, their language does not seem exactly like the ecstatic prayers Paul attributes to the Corinthians. It seems to resemble more closely the language of inspired canticles, such as the song in which Mary "magnifies (*megalynei*) the Lord" (Luke 1:46) and proclaims: "He who is mighty has done great things (*megala*) for me" (v. 49). Under the influence of the Spirit, the apostles began to praise God and to sing his marvelous deeds, as one day the victors over evil will sing in the final song of triumph: "Great (*megala*) and admirable are your works, Lord God Almighty" (Revelation 15:3). The first effect of the Spirit, who fills the apostles' hearts, is to make them overflow with admiration and gratitude to God. These sentiments are spontaneously expressed in hymns, which are a form of prophecy, not of glossolalia. This feature of the Pentecost narrative makes it easier for us to understand why the oracle of Joel is applied to the situation depicted there, for Joel announces an outpouring of the Spirit which will cause all who receive it to prophesy (Acts 2:17-18).

Thus, despite some similarities with the gift of "tongues" as described in other texts, it is apparent that the charism the Spirit gave the apostles at Pentecost was of a different type, and that it more closely resembled the genre of prophecy, as exemplified by inspired canticles.

In Other Tongues

A. In Caesarea and Ephesus, as in Corinth, we hear of "speaking in tongues," but the Pentecost narrative mentions "speaking in *other* tongues." Luke may have a special reason for using the adjective "other" here, whereas he felt no such need to use it in texts such as 10:46 and 19:6.

The adjective "other" (*heteros*) is typical of Luke's vocabulary. In contrast to only one occurrence in Mark (16:12 in the appendix), eight in Matthew, and one in John, we find this adjective no less than thirty-two times in Luke's Gospel and seventeen times in Acts. In the episode of the transfiguration, for example, where the other Synoptics state that Jesus "was transfigured before them" (Mark 9:2; Matthew 17:2), Luke writes: "As he was praying, the appearance of his face became *other*."

The nuance of the adjective varies with the context. In the example given, Jesus' appearance became "other," that is, different from what it usually was. In the prologue to Ben Sirach, the adjective modifies the noun *glossa*: the author's grandson remarks that it is difficult to translate Hebrew "into another language," i.e., into a foreign tongue (Ecclesiasticus 1:22). We may also recall Isaiah 28:11, which Paul quotes to the Corinthians: God threatens Israel that he will speak to it through triumphant foes, whose language it will not understand: "I will speak to this people through men of another tongue (*en heteroglossois*) and through lips of strangers (*heteron*)" (1 Corinthians 14:21). "Another tongue" normally means a foreign language.

B. At the end of the verse we have been considering, Luke adds one more specific detail: *as the Spirit gave them the power to speak.* Lucan style is evident in the use of the conjunction "as, according to" (*kathos*) and in the construction of the verb "to give" with an infinitive following. The verb "to speak" in this phrase (*apophtheggomai*) reappears in only two other passages within the New Testament, in Acts 2:14 and 26:25; the translation does not bring out its full force, for it suggests speech that is especially solemn and inspired. In 2:14 this verb introduces Peter's great discourse, which clearly belongs to a different category than the "speaking in tongues" mentioned earlier; in 26:25 the same verb suggests the qualities of common sense and truth in Paul's defense before Agrippa. The use that Luke makes of this verb in other contexts, therefore, encourages us to conclude that when the apostles "spoke in other tongues, as the Spirit gave them the power to speak," they were talking in a perfectly intelligible way.

C. Finally and above all, it is not legitimate to interpret verse 4 in isolation, that is, without taking into account *the evidence provided by the following verses.* After mentioning that the apostles "spoke in other tongues," Luke goes on to describe the reaction of those who were present. The first detail he gives is that "everyone heard them speaking (*lalounton*) in his own language" (v. 6). The next verses emphasize the anomaly of the situation: that "these men who are speaking (*hoi lalountes*) are all Galileans," and yet each one of the witnesses "hears them in his own language" (vv. 7-8). And after the enumeration of the peoples represented in the crowd, the same idea is stressed a third time: "We hear them speaking (*lalounton*) in our own tongues of the marvelous works of God" (v. 11). The narrative leaves no doubt about the meaning of the expression that we are trying to define: "to speak in other tongues" means precisely "to speak in the very language (*dialekton*)" of each auditor (vv. 6, 8), or, as they put it themselves, "to speak in our own tongues" (v. 11). This fact amazes them because they know that "those who speak are all Galileans" (v. 7). The surprising thing is not that Galileans, rather than another group, start "speaking in tongues." The surprise arises from the fact that men who are all of one language (in this case, "all Galileans") are heard speaking a great number of languages.

Sometimes another theory is propounded, namely that the apostles' speech was unintelligible in itself, but that the Holy Spirit made their utterances miraculously intelligible to the auditors, so that each was able to hear them in his own mother tongue. Adherents of this hypothesis emphasize the repeated use of the verb "to hear": "each one *heard* them speaking his own language" (v. 6); "each of us *hears* them in his own language" (v. 8); "we *hear* them speaking in our own tongues" (v. 11). But this theory is not easy to reconcile with the narrative as we have it; it is ruled out by the equally frequent but more emphatic presence of the verb "to speak" (*lalein*) in the text. When we put the question correctly—when we ask "What did Luke wish his readers to understand?"—no doubt seems possible. Luke really intended to convey the impression that the apostles spoke in the languages of the different peoples to which the witnesses of this event belonged.

One problem remains. It is necessary to reconcile the obvious sense of the narrative, taken as a whole, with those features of the story which seem to allude to the gift of tongues as it appeared in Caesarea, Ephesus and Corinth. We have already mentioned that many authors feel no need to reconcile such details, for they imagine that Luke has simply amalgamated, more or less felicitously, two quite different versions of the same event. Or they may suppose that Luke has superimposed on an earlier form of the story a later interpretation which does not really fit: thus the charism that enabled the apostles to "speak in tongues" has been transformed by an editorial process into a more marvelous and more richly symbolic gift that empowers them to "speak in other tongues."

However, Luke has clearly put his personal stamp on the entire Pentecost narrative. And that fact alone should encourage us to give greater weight to a single intention on his part, an intention that unifies his whole presentation. If certain features remind us, as they do, of the gift of tongues, we may attribute that to the fact that Luke imagines the Pentecost event along the lines of manifestations of the Spirit that are more familiar to him. Yet the analogy with the gift of tongues remains secondary for Luke. He emphasizes the difference between them far more than the resemblance. The apostles did not speak "in tongues," but "in other tongues," in foreign tongues. They praised God among the nations (Romans 15:9; Psalm 18:50) and in the different languages of those nations.

III. ALL THE NATIONS UNDER HEAVEN

Now there were Jews living in Jerusalem, devout men from all the nations under heaven. At the sound, a multitude gathered, bewildered because each of them heard them speaking in his own language. They were amazed, and in their astonishment they said, "Are not these men who are speaking all Galileans? How is it that each of us hears them in his own mother tongue? Parthians, Medes and Elamites, inhabitants of Mesopotamia, of Judea and Cappadocia, of Pontus and Asia, of Phrygia and Pamphylia, of Egypt and the part of Libya close to Cyrene, visitors from Rome, Jews as well as proselytes, Cretans and Arabs, we hear them praising the mighty works of God in our own tongues (vv. 5-11).

The Amazement of the Multitude

The "resounding noise" mentioned in verse 2 is recalled in verse 6 by the more general term "sound, noise." This sound has not only "filled the whole house" (v. 2), but it has also been heard outside. A crowd gathers, and the apostles are discovered "speaking in other tongues." Notice at this point the way that Luke emphasizes the amazement produced by the apostles' speech.

The crowd is first described as "bewildered," in utter confusion. The same term will recur later in Acts to characterize the disorder of the crowd in Ephesus, stirred up by the goldsmiths (19:29, 32), and still later in connection with the uproar in Jerusalem at the time of Paul's arrest (21:31). The way the scene is described reminds us that the story is set in the East. Westerners would probably just stand and gape. In the East, amazement is translated into motion, wild gestures and exclamations.

The remark "They were amazed, and in their astonishment they said. ..." (v. 7) will be repeated below: "They were all amazed, and, full of perplexity, they said to one another. ..." (v. 12). Their amazement is spontaneously expressed in words: "How does it happen that each of us hears them in his own mother tongue? ... We hear them speaking in our own tongues. ... What does this mean?" (vv. 8, 11, 12).

The reader may wonder why Luke emphasizes this feature so deliberately. Several considerations appear to have motivated him. First of all, the amazement of the crowd testifies, indirectly but quite effectively, to the extraordinary nature of the event; the immediate witnesses realized that they had encountered a phenomenon that could not be explained in purely human terms. Secondly, the remarks of the crowd prepare us, from a literary point of view, for Peter's speech to follow; the crowd's amazement calls for the explanation that Peter will give. Finally, and on a deeper level, astonishment is the prelude to faith. That is one reason why the evangelists, especially Luke, often mention astonishment in the same context as fear. Astonishment and fear are man's initial reactions when confronted with a divine revelation, his spontaneous responses before the supernatural.

These spontaneous reactions are not in themselves specifically religious, but they can lead to properly religious experience if we discover a religious meaning in the extraordinary phenomenon we have encountered and perceive in it an appeal that requires a personal response on our part. That response will be faith. Thus miracles do not of themselves produce faith, but they prepare for it. In many cases further explanations are required, such as Peter's demonstration at Pentecost that the event they are witnessing is the fulfillment of a promise that concerns those who are listening to him (vv. 16ff., 38ff.). Amazement is a stage preliminary to faith; its divinely intended purpose is realized when listeners, previously bewildered, "welcome the word" of salvation (v. 41).

Devout Jews

Luke does not call the assembled people precisely a "crowd"; he prefers another word, a favorite of his: "the multitude" (*plethos*). In connection with this, we might recall the promise made by God to Abraham to make him the father of a "multitude" of peoples, a promise that led to a change of his name from Abram ("exalted father") to Abraham ("father of a multitude") (Genesis 17:4-5; cf. Deuteronomy 26:5; Hebrews 11:12). That promise seemed to have been realized already when Israel arrived at Mount Sinai (cf. Deuteronomy 1:10; 10:22), but the coming of the Spirit at Pentecost will give it a still more marvelous fulfillment. Another passage worth recalling is the description Luke gives us of Jesus' audience at the Sermon on the Plain: "Present was a great crowd of his disciples, and a great multitude of people from all Judea and Jerusalem and the seacoast of Tyre and Sidon, who came to listen to him" (Luke 6:17; cf. Mark 3:7-8). The audience at Pentecost reminds us, though on a larger scale, of this audience that Jesus knew at the beginning of his ministry.

All of these people are *Jews*, and so Peter's speech will be addressed to "men of Judea" (v. 14). Luke specifies that they are "devout men" (*andres eulabeis*) (v. 5), and the adjective used here expresses the idea of a piety essentially composed of fear of God and concern to carry out scrupulously "the prescriptions and observances of the Lord" (cf. Luke 1:6). This adjective characterizes a religious attitude that is typically Jewish and applies only to Jews (cf. Luke 2:25; Acts 8:2; 22:12). Yet beside those who are "Jews" by birth, there are also "proselytes" present in the crowd (v. 11), individuals born in paganism, but converted to Judaism with all its obligations, including circumcision.

Of all of these Jews, by birth or at least by religion, we are told that they were "dwelling in Jerusalem" (v. 5). As the sequel shows that they were born elsewhere, we must conclude that they had settled in the Holy City. As for the "Romans" mentioned in the list, they are specifically said to be "residents" (v. 10); hence they are Jews, originally from Rome, who had later come to live in Jerusalem, while perhaps retaining their status as foreigners. They may be identified, at least in part, with the *libertini*, the "freedmen," whose synagogue is mentioned in Acts 6:9. Hence it follows that Peter's audience on Pentecost was composed of people who had settled in Jerusalem, and nothing in Luke's narrative would suggest that they were pilgrims who had simply come for the feast. Furthermore, there is no mention in Acts, prior to chapter 8, of any expansion of Christianity outside of Jerusalem, and we have no reason to imagine the converts made at Pentecost as scattering a few days later to go back to faraway homes. Just as, thirty years earlier, a devout old man and a pious widow of Jerusalem were the ones who welcomed the child Jesus at his first arrival in the Holy City (Luke 2:25, 37), so likewise at Pentecost the message of the New Covenant was publicly announced for the first time to Jews, whose piety had led them to settle in the shadow of the temple.

From All Nations

The text says of these Jews of Jerusalem that they came literally "from every nation of those that are under heaven," that is,
"from every nation on earth." The word "nation" (*ethnos*) in this
context obviously does not designate an ethnic group. The Jews
who are mentioned here belonged to one or other "nation" in the
sense that they were part of the population occupying the region
that bore the name of the nation in question, but that does not
mean that ethnically they had ceased being Jews.

Luke uses a rather solemn formula: "all the nations that are
under heaven." This formulation may remind us of a saying of
Jesus that is preserved in the Gospels. Matthew's version is simply:
"The nations [the Gentiles] worry about all these things" (Matthew
6:32), such as food and clothing. But the saying is slightly different
in Luke's version: "About these things *all the nations of the world*
worry" (Luke 12:30). The expression also brings to mind the statement of Deuteronomy 2:25: "Today, I begin to spread the dread
and fear of you over the face of all the nations that are under
heaven. . . ." Hence Luke's formula is "biblical" in its style and may
also be intended to suggest the fulfillment of the promise that
assured Israel of the submission of all nations.

The statement in verse 5 is illustrated by the list contained in
verses 9-11. This list obviously does not pretend to be exhaustive,
for we know that the peoples of the earth, according to the Jewish
theory based on Genesis 10, are seventy in number (and that is the
reason the rabbis imagined that God's voice divided on Sinai into
seventy voices). The enumeration starts with the Parthians, who
represent the Eastern extremity of the world; next come the Medes
and Elamites, who are situated north of the Persian Gulf; then the
inhabitants of Mesopotamia, that is, those who had come from the
country between the Tigris and the Euphrates. Instead of continuing toward the West by mentioning Cappadocia and Pontus at this
point, the list now inserts Judea, which is entirely out of place here;
we can only conjecture about the term that the text must originally
have contained. (Was it Armenia? Or Syria?) In any case, several
regions of what we call Asia Minor are mentioned next: Cappadocia
(in the west), Pontus (in the north), Asia (the ancient Ionian coast),

Phrygia (in western Asia), Pamphylia (with Perga, on the southern coast). Then all of a sudden we pass to Egypt and Libya close to Cyrene, and on to Rome. The enumeration seems to be over when we find the clarifying remark, "Jews as well as proselytes," which naturally applies to the entire series. But then, as an afterthought, allusion is suddenly made to Cretans and Arabs as well.

This enumeration has always amazed commentators by what it includes, and even more by what it omits. It is noteworthy that all the peoples named, except the Romans, belong to the eastern Mediterranean, and that even Greece is too far west to be included. The list mentions regions of little importance, such as Pamphylia, while omitting more important ones, like Cilicia (eastward of Pamphylia); Crete is included, but not Cyprus. At least one thing about the list is perfectly clear, namely that it corresponds so little with Luke's own geographical horizons that he surely did not compose it himself. He must have found it somewhere and inserted it more or less intact into his text. The insertion, however, disrupts the unity of Luke's composition, to such an extent that he is forced to repeat again in verses 11b-12a what he has already said in verses 7-8.

It is not difficult to guess Luke's motive in inserting this material. The catalogue of place names is integrated into an obviously fictitious conversation, a literary form of which Luke is fond. The purpose of the conversation is to make clear to the readers of Acts that "all the nations that are under heaven" were really represented among the Jews who made up Peter's audience at Pentecost. For this purpose it was not necessary that the list be exhaustive, but it was useful to include a few out of the way and unimportant nations, to show that even they were represented in Jerusalem. In a certain sense the whole universe was present, symbolically, to witness the coming of the Spirit and hear the word of God.

This universalist outlook which we discover in the Pentecost narrative is, of course, a characteristic feature of Luke's writings. Early in his Gospel, he quotes the promise of the prophet Isaiah that "all flesh shall see the salvation of God" (Isaiah 40:5; Luke 3:6), and the Acts of the Apostles closes with a statement by Paul that recalls the same oracle of Isaiah: "Be it known to you that this salvation of God has been sent to the nations" (Acts 28:28). Luke chooses to conclude his Gospel with a statement by Jesus which reminds us that, according to the Scriptures, the message of forgiveness must be "announced to all nations, beginning from Jerusalem" (Luke 24:27), and at the beginning of Acts he gives us a more detailed statement by Jesus, just before his ascension: "You will be my witnesses in Jerusalem, in the whole of Judea and Samaria, and even to the ends of the earth" (Acts 1:8). This same universalist perspective is expressed at the end of Paul's inaugural discourse in which he explicitly refers to an oracle of Isaiah: "I have established you as a light to the nations, to carry salvation to the ends of the earth" (Isaiah 49:6; Acts 13:47).

Luke's Pentecost narrative acquires its full meaning when it is seen, as Luke intended it to be, within this wider perspective. Obviously Luke could not say that all the pagan nations had been evangelized as of that first moment in his story; the time for the mission to the Gentiles will come only later. Nevertheless, among the Jews who gathered together at the coming of the Spirit, Luke is happy to point out representatives of all nations, thus suggesting in broad outline the universality of the apostles' mission. The history of the expansion of Christianity will merely be the logical consequence of the universal orientation that the Church received from the Holy Spirit from the very first day.

The Church was born universal. She has no other limits than the world: "unto the ends of the earth." The light she possesses is to illuminate all peoples. Salvation is entrusted to her so that she may hand it on. In the last analysis, that is the meaning of the Pentecost miracle: the Spirit gives the whole world to the Church, thus imposing on her the immense missionary effort by which she will reach her fullness and her eschatological stature.

IV. CONCLUSION

At the end of this study it may be useful to summarize the principal features we have discovered in the Pentecost narrative in Acts:

A. The Holy Spirit came upon the apostles on the feast day at which Judaism commemorated the promulgation of the Law and the creation of the Covenant between God and his people gathered in "assembly" (*ekklesia*; cf. Acts 7:38). The Christian Pentecost, which celebrates the Spirit's coming, commemorates a New Covenant, which created a new people of God and constituted them a Church. This Covenant is not based, like the old one, on the regulations of a Law imposed on men from without; it is based on the Spirit, who transforms hearts and inspires a filial attitude toward God.

B. The mystery of Pentecost concerns "all the nations that are under heaven." Certain Jewish traditions had already attributed a universal significance to the events on Sinai: theoretically the divine Law was destined for all peoples. Practically, however, only Israel had received the Law, and it was necessary to be incorporated into Israel in order to become a member of the people of God. The economy of the Spirit, on the other hand, is characterized by real and effective universality. This universal character, though present as early as Pentecost morning, could be realized only by progressive stages, as the testimony of the apostles spread "to the ends of the earth." The essential universality of the Church born of the Spirit implies and imposes a call to missionary activity. The Church will be a missionary Church until the end of time.

C. On Pentecost morning the universality of the Church found concrete expression in the gift that enabled the apostles to "speak in other tongues," in the particular language of every people to which they would have to bring their testimony. Though rabbinic legends imagined a similar phenomenon on Mount Sinai, the undeniable fact was that the Law had come to men in Hebrew clothing, and Hebrew, as the langage of revelation, became a sacred language. The Christian Church will no longer be tied to a single tongue, whether it be the Hebrew of its forefathers, the Aramaic spoken by Jesus and the first apostles, or the Greek of the inspired authors of the New Testament. The languages and the cultures of all peoples are given by the Spirit to the apostles and through them to the Church. The economy of the Spirit no longer tolerates the supremacy of one tongue or a single culture above others; rather it appropriates them all. From now on it will be unnecessary to become a Jew in order to enjoy the blessings of the Covenant; it will no longer be necessary to adopt the language or the customs of any one people rather than another. It will be enough to listen to the Spirit speaking and follow his inspirations.

Conversion in the
Acts of the Apostles

The history of the apostolic Church is a story of growth, sometimes in rapid leaps forward, sometimes at a slower but steady pace. There are great hauls. On Pentecost "some three thousand persons were added" to the Christian community (Acts 2:41), and after the healing of the cripple about five thousand men embraced the faith (4:4). There are also the day-by-day conversions. "Each day the Lord added to the community those who were to be saved" (2:47). "More and more believers adhered to the Lord, a multitude of men and women" (5:14). "The word of the Lord grew, the number of disciples increased considerably in Jerusalem, and a multitude of priests accepted the faith" (6:7). Before long the movement spreads beyond Jerusalem, and soon the Church includes thriving communities all over Judea, Samaria, Galilee and Phoenicia, at Antioch, on the island of Cyprus, in Asia Minor, in Greece, in Puteoli, and in Rome. When we consider this astonishing expansion, we cannot help wondering what motivated these conversions. And since alongside the many who accepted the message there were also many who rejected it, what accounts for a conversion in one case and not in another?

The extraordinary picture of missionary experience contained in the Acts of the Apostles furnishes abundant evidence about the early Christian understanding of conversion, its normal conditions, and its various determining factors. Three considerations seem basic in early Christian thinking about conversion, and they provide us with three subheadings under which we may organize the evidence from Acts. First of all, there is genuine hope for conversion only in the case of persons who have a *sense of their sinfulness* before God and are anxious to obtain God's forgiveness. Secondly, conversion to Christianity is essentially and specifically related to *the mystery of Easter*, for the same power that God revealed in Jesus' resurrection continues acting in our own present and in our future. Finally, conversion implies a *change of life*, an acceptance of the special lifestyle of the Christian community.

I. THE SENSE OF SIN

The preacher of the Good News may find himself in two different situations. If his hearers already know that they are sinners, all he has to do is invite them to *believe* and promise them the forgiveness of their sins. But if his audience is made up of people who have no awareness of their sinfulness before God, then his first task will be to bring them to this awareness. His approach in this second case will vary depending on whether he is addressing a pagan audience or a Jewish one, but his goal in either case will be the same: to lead his hearers to repentance.

Faith and the Forgiveness of Sins

In his speech to Cornelius, the centurion from Caesarea, Peter gives us a summary of early Christian preaching that follows the outline of the Gospel narratives, mentioning in order the good deeds of Jesus during his earthly life, the circumstances of his death, his resurrection, and the appearances to the apostles who were commanded to announce the coming of the last judgment. Then Peter concludes his speech with an invitation to believe, couched in these terms:

> He [Jesus] is the one of whom the prophets testify that everyone who believes in him will receive, through his name, the remission of his sins (10:43).

Thus in order to lead Cornelius to faith, Peter emphasizes its possible advantage to him, namely that faith will procure pardon from his sins. This abrupt allusion to Cornelius' sinfulness may take us by surprise. Peter has not prepared us for it by any mention of the centurion's sins prior to this point in the discourse. And Luke's introductory description of him, far from emphasizing his blame-worthiness, presents him as a pious and God-fearing person, assiduous in almsgiving and prayer (10:2). On the other hand, of course, it is precisely in a religious man such as the centurion that we expect to find a sensitive conscience. In any case, Peter tries to draw him to faith by promising him God's forgiveness, and this supposes that Cornelius will know he is a sinner and desire to be forgiven.

Paul strikes a similar note in his speech to the Jews at Antioch in Pisidia. His presentation of the Christian message on that occasion leads up to this final declaration:

> Be it known to you, brethren, that it is by this man [Jesus] that remission of sins is proclaimed to you. Through him everyone who believes receives the total justification which you were unable to obtain through the Law of Moses (13:38).

Paul's reasoning here supposes an awareness among his hearers that, since the Law was not able to justify them, they are still in sin and in need of God's forgiveness. Building on their sense of sin, Paul may be able to awaken their interest in the faith and draw them to faith as the means by which they will obtain God's pardon.

In another speech, this time before King Agrippa, Paul describes the mission that Christ entrusted to him on the road to Damascus and quotes Christ's own mandate to him:

> I am sending you to the pagan nations to open their eyes, so that they may turn from darkness to light, from the dominion of Satan to God, and that they may, through faith in me, receive forgiveness of their sins and a share in the inheritance of the sanctified (26:17-18).

In this text, too, it is the promise of pardon and of a share in the inheritance of the world to come which is expected to attract men to faith. The promise applies, however, only to those who are aware of their guilt and desire forgiveness.

On the road to Damascus, Saul the persecutor became Paul the apostle. From the viewpoint of literary genre, the account of this event in Acts is closer to a vocation story than to a conversion narrative. Nevertheless, Paul's vocation does involve a conversion. The words of the old man Ananias, which Paul reports in his speech to the crowd in Jerusalem, remind us of normal conversion-language. Ananias tells Paul, "Be baptized, and wash away your sins by calling on his name" (22:16). Those receiving baptism did, in fact, call on the name of Jesus while professing their faith in him as Lord, and Ananias attributes the power of forgiving sins directly to this baptismal profession of faith. In inviting Paul to make this act of faith and at the same time promising him forgiveness, Ananias seems to suppose that Paul is conscious of his sinfulness and desires forgiveness.

The four passages we have just considered reveal a common conviction: the call to faith always implies awareness of sin and desire for pardon. This underlying conviction will emerge even more clearly in the texts with which we are about to deal. All of them depict the effort expended by the apostles to induce various groups of hearers to acknowledge their sinfulness.

The Pagans and their Sin

One source of inspiration for Paul's speech before the Areopagus in Athens is the stock items of Jewish invective against pagan religion. Though Paul does not spell out these traditional accusations in any great detail, they are easy for us to recognize, especially in his critical remarks about temples as the imagined dwelling places of the divine (17:24), about sacrifices as supposedly satisfying real needs of the gods (v. 25), and about statues which are not sufficiently distinguished from the deity they represent (v. 29). Hence Paul logically ends his discourse with a call to repentance: "God has overlooked the times of ignorance, but now he commands all men everywhere to repent" (v. 30). The behavior of the pagans betrays a culpable "ignorance" of God on their part, and the word "ignorance" connotes here, as it does in Jewish usage, a deliberate failure to acknowledge the true God. Pagan worship is offensive to God, as the stereotyped reproaches in the body of the discourse are intended to make clear, and that is the reason why Paul invites his audience to "repent." Since they have sinned before the unique and living God, they must now obtain his forgiveness, and to receive forgiveness they must repent.

We have already seen an instance of Peter's preaching before a pagan audience, and we will recall that Peter, in addressing the centurion at Caesarea, urged him to believe in order to receive forgiveness of his sins, but that he did not apparently make much of Cornelius' sinfulness or reproach him for any specific sin. However, we encounter a slightly different mentality among the Christians at Jerusalem whom Peter meets on his return. From his recital of the Cornelius story, they draw the following significant conclusion: "Therefore to the Gentiles also God has granted *repentance* that leads to life" (11:18). Obviously they are reasoning like Jews, and therefore they consider Cornelius, precisely because he is a pagan, to be a sinner, excluded from eternal life. Therefore his conversion necessarily appears to them as an act of repentance.

Paul employs a similar Jewish mode of expression in describing his own ministry:

> First to the inhabitants of Damascus, next to those of Jerusalem and the whole land of Judea, and then to the pagans, I declared that they should repent and turn to God by doing works befitting repentance (26:20).

The terms used here apply in their proper sense mainly to the content of Paul's preaching to the pagans. The appeal to "turn to God" is addressed to them, and so is the appeal to "repent," since they are guilty, as pagans, in the sight of God.

Elsewhere he reports the content of his preaching at Ephesus in the following terms: "I urged Jews and Greeks to repent toward God and to believe in the Lord Jesus" (20:21). When speaking to Jews, Paul tries to bring them to faith in the Lord Jesus. But pagans he asks "to repent toward God"—an unusual abbreviated form of the expression "to repent and turn toward God." Even when the apostolic preaching does not make a special point of the pagans' sinfulness, yet it spontaneously conceives their conversion as an act of repentance, so evident is it to the Jewish mind that all pagans are sinners.

The case of Simon the magician illustrates the same complex of ideas. Simon imagined that it would be possible to "buy the gift of God with money" (8:20), a fault for which Peter sharply reproaches him:

> Your heart is not right before God. Repent of your wicked purpose, and pray the Lord so as to obtain pardon for this thought of your heart (vv. 21-22).

Thus here, too, we find the same sequence: an offense against God, a remonstrance which brings the sin to light, and an invitation to the repentance by which pardon can be won.

In brief, the appeal to repentance is always addressed to sinners, and repentance is the precise form of conversion expected of them. Even to be able to hear this appeal, people must already realize their sinfulness. Hence the apostolic preaching, when addressed to pagans, incorporated arguments that Judaism had already been using for some time to demonstrate the sinfulness of pagan worship, and the sin of Simon the magician is rather similar to that of the pagans. Before conversion is possible in such cases the persons addressed must be persuaded that every deviation of religious feeling into the paths of idolatry or superstition is an offense against God. Once that has been explained, the preacher may then invite his listeners, not so much directly "to believe" or "to be converted," but more precisely "to repent."

The People of Jerusalem and Their Sin

Each of Peter's speeches in Jerusalem contains extremely strong accusations against the audience. This may seem to be a strange approach on the part of a missionary who is looking for conversions, as Peter certainly is. Yet these reproaches do serve his purpose, for they jolt the hearers into awareness of the sin that weighs them down, and thus dispose them to listen to Peter's concluding appeal for conversion. The charge he lays against them is always the same: the inhabitants of Jerusalem are responsible for the death of Jesus.

This is the way the accusation is worded in the speech at Pentecost:

> Jesus of Nazareth, the man whom God accredited to you by the
> miracles, signs and portents which he worked through him in your
> midst ... you took and put him to death, getting the pagans to nail
> him to the cross ... but God has made him Lord and Messiah, this
> Jesus whom you crucified (2:22-23, 36).

Despite God's own testimony in Jesus' favor by the many miracles
worked through his hands, the people of Jerusalem unhesitatingly
resolved to kill him, and even went so far as to appeal to godless
pagans for help in putting him to death. Their crime touched God
himself directly, as he showed by personally intervening to bring
back from the dead the one whom they had killed. Peter's indict-
ment produced the desired effect on his audience, for "on hearing
this, they were cut to the heart, and said to Peter and the apostles,
'Brethren, what are we to do?'" (v. 37). At this point they are
ready to listen, and Peter makes his final appeal: "Repent, and let
everyone among you be baptized in the name of Jesus Christ for the
forgiveness of his sins" (v. 38). This appeal to conversion, coming
as it does here after the emphatic reminder of their sinfulness before
God, takes the form of an appeal for repentance.

The accusations are even more vehement in Peter's speech
after the healing of the cripple at the Beautiful Gate:

> The God of our fathers has glorified his servant Jesus, whom you
> delivered and denied before Pilate, when he had made up his mind to
> set him free. You repudiated the one who was holy and just; you
> begged for the release of a murderer, while you put the Prince of life
> to death. ... Yet, brothers, I know that you acted in ignorance, as did
> your rulers. ... Repent, therefore, and be converted, so that your sins
> may be wiped out (3:13-14, 17, 19).

The sin they have committed is so enormous that his listeners
might despair of forgiveness, but Peter heads off that reaction. He
points to their ignorance as an excusing factor. Peter's concern is
obviously not to assuage their guilt-feelings, but to remind them
that forgiveness is still possible for them. The condition for forgiveness will be repentance.

Responsibility for Calvary must be shared by both the common
people of Jerusalem and by their leaders, the members of the Sanhedrin. But the major share of the responsibility lies with the latter,

and Peter is not afraid to tell them so. At his first appearance before the Sanhedrin, he declares: "You crucified Jesus Christ of Nazareth. ... He is the stone which you, the builders, rejected" (4:10-11), and the allusion to prophecies in Peter's accusation emphasizes the seriousness of the sin involved. His speech ends, however, on a promise: "There is no other name under heaven given to men by which we are to be saved" (v. 12), the wording of which reminds us of the prophecy, "He who invokes the name of the Lord will be saved" (Joel 3:5, cited also in Acts 2:21). The contrast between the accusation and the promise in this text is certainly deliberate. Though Peter is in no position to deliver a direct exhortation to his judges, he does what he can to suggest to them that their sin need not go unforgiven.

The condition of this forgiveness Peter expresses more clearly in his discourse at his second appearance before the Sanhedrin:

> The God of our fathers has raised this Jesus, whom you put to death by hanging him on a gibbet. He it is whom God exalted to his right hand, making him Leader and Savior, to grant Israel through him repentance and forgiveness of sins (5:30-31).

Despite the gravity of the offenses committed against him, God is ready to forgive, but this requires repentance—or, to put it more precisely, this requires that those who are guilty of sin open their hearts to the grace of repentance that God grants them through the risen Christ.

The sin of the people of Jerusalem became a commonplace theme in the apostolic preaching, and it reappears in some contexts in which its original purpose appears to have been forgotten. Peter alludes to it, for instance, in his speech in the home of Cornelius:

> We are witness of all that he did in the land of the Jews and in Jerusalem, he whom they went so far as to put to death by hanging on the gibbet (10:39).

We discover the same theme also in Paul's speech to the Jews at Antioch in Pisidia:

> The inhabitants of Jerusalem and their leaders unknowingly fulfilled the words of the prophets which are read every Sabbath: though they

had not found grounds for death in him, yet they condemned him and asked Pilate to have him executed (13:27-28)

When we come upon texts of this nature in our reading, it is helpful to recall the original purpose of accusations like these. They were not motivated by barren hostility toward the Jews. The reproaches leveled against the Jews function within the setting of the speeches in Acts just as similar reproaches addressed to their own people by the Old Testament prophets functioned in their original contexts. Their purpose is to call the listeners back to self-awareness and awaken in them dispositions of compunction leading to forgiveness.

In summary, Peter reminds his original listeners of the details of the passion in order to lead them to repentance and conversion. Of course, recollection of Jesus' passion serves a purpose for others as well. From the prophecy of the Suffering Servant and from the teaching of the Lord himself, the apostolic community knew that Jesus had died for our sins and to redeem from their sins the whole human collectivity. On a deeper level of causality, our sins too nailed Jesus to the cross; the inhabitants of Jerusalem and Pilate's soldiers were only the executioners. Who would dare throw stones at them? Who can claim to be innocent of this blood? If the apostolic preaching did not explicitly draw this conclusion, at least it stated the premises from which we may legitimately draw it ourselves. We remain faithful to the spirit of .the early preaching when we contemplate the details of Jesus' passion in such a way as to grow increasingly aware of the ugliness of sin and arouse in ourselves that sincere repentance to which the promise of forgiveness is tied.

II. The Paschal Mystery

In the first group of texts which we have been examining, conversion follows upon an awareness of sin and takes the form of repentance (*metanoia*). In the texts that we are going to study now, conversion will appear in a more positive light, as an act by which a person "turns" (*epistrephein*) toward God or toward the Lord. We shall also see in particular that the "turning" involved in conversion is specifically related to the Easter event, considered in all its temporal dimensions, that is, as an event of the past, the present and the future.

Turning toward God, and Turning toward the Lord

To describe what happens at the conversion of pagans, the early Christians employed an older Jewish expression and spoke of "turning away from idols and toward the true God." Paul uses this expression in his First Letter to the Thessalonians; in the pertinent passage he wants to remind them of their initial response to his preaching, and in the process we find him spontaneously echoing the very language with which he first addressed them:

You turned toward God, [turning away] from idols, to put yourselves at the service of the living and true God (1:9).

Likewise Paul in Acts tells the pagans at Lystra:

We bring you the Good News that you are to turn away from all these vain idols in order to turn toward the living God who made the heavens, the earth, the sea, and everything in them (14:15).

Unlike the idols, which are material objects with no life or movement, the true God is a God who lives and acts, as he has demonstrated by creating everything that exists, and as he continues to demonstrate by the blessings he bestows on his creatures (v. 17). "To turn" toward him means to acknowledge him as the only true God, to give him the worship that he alone deserves, or, in Paul's language to the Thessalonians, "to put oneself at his service." Finally, we find a further example of the Jewish expression we are considering in another passage in Acts, in which James urges Jewish Christians not to create unnecessary difficulties for "those among the pagans who turn to God" (15:19).

Thus Christians merely take over the formula that the Jews used to describe the conversion of pagans to the one true God of Israel; the only difference is that the same expression is now applied to pagans who accept the message of the Gospel. Paul, however, gives us a fuller description of the conversion process; we are in the context of his defense before Agrippa, and Paul is reporting the missionary mandate that he received directly from Jesus:

> I am sending you to the pagan nations, that you may open their eyes, so that they may turn from darkness to the light, and from the dominion of Satan to God (26:18).

Paul's language here is obviously influenced by Isaiah 42:7, 16; he compares the convert to a blind man who recovers his sight, passing from darkness to light. In a second metaphor he also compares him to a person who has left behind the camp of Satan, the realm where Satan rules, to pass over into the camp of God. The same basic notion of a return to the true God is present in this text, but Paul has developed the idea in a more pictorial and imaginative way.

The expression "turning toward the Lord" has exactly the same meaning in Jewish usage as the other expression "turning toward God"; the only difference is that the title "Lord" replaces "Yahweh" which is the proper name of the God of Israel. Christians, on the other hand, tend to reserve the title "Lord" for the risen Jesus, and therefore in Acts the expression "turning toward the Lord" denotes a conversion to Christianity, adherence to the Lord Jesus. Luke consistently applies the title "Lord" in this way. For example, he mentions that the missionaries who came to Antioch did not hesitate to "speak also to the Greeks, announcing to them the Good News of the Lord Jesus" (11:20), and that as a result of their preaching "the hand of the Lord was with them, and great was the number of those who, embracing the faith, turned toward the Lord" (v. 21). The Lord to whom these pagans of Antioch are converted is the same one who is announced to them in the preaching: the Lord Jesus. Elsewhere in Acts Luke reports that, as a result of a miraculous healing performed by Peter, "all the inhabitants of Lydda and of the plain of Sharon were converted to the Lord" (9:35); Peter's words to the paralytic earlier in this context already make sufficiently clear who "the Lord" in question is: "Aeneas, Jesus Christ heals you" (v. 34).

These few passages have focused our attention on the most basic feature of conversion, namely that it consists in turning toward somebody: toward God or the Lord Jesus. Hence being converted does not mean subscribing to a system of doctrines. It does mean accepting a person; it involves adhering to the living God, and to Jesus whom we confess as Lord. We must now consider another aspect of the subject and attempt to show that conversion, thus understood, is essentially related to the event of Easter.

The Resurrection, a Past Event
Continuing into the Present

Whenever the apostles have occasion to speak about the sin of the inhabitants of Jerusalem in putting Jesus to death, they immediately go on to assert: "But God raised him up!" The declaration "God raised Jesus" occurs repeatedly and in the same form from the beginning of the Acts of the Apostles to the end. It constitutes the essential core of the Christian message. The living God whom Christians acknowledge is not only the God who created heaven and earth, but also and even primarily the God who raised Jesus up. The Lord they turned to when they became Christians is Jesus, whom God raised from the dead to seat him at his own right hand (2:34-36).

The conviction that God really raised Jesus is grounded, first of all, on the testimony of the apostles who saw Jesus alive after Easter and ate and drank with him. Yet the testimony of the apostles, important though it be, might be insufficient by itself, that is, if God had not intervened personally to testify on behalf of the risen Christ. That personal intervention takes two forms: first of all, miracles, and secondly, the action of God's grace.

Miracles. The first miracle after Easter is that of Pentecost. The coming of the Spirit is signaled by an uproar and the ecstasy of the apostles. This draws a crowd, some of whom are struck with amazement, while others are moved to mockery. But these phenomena, extraordinary though they may be, do not of themselves produce conversions. Before these miraculous events can have any effect on the innermost hearts of the bystanders, they must first be recognized as signs from God. It is precisely the function of Peter's speech to give the required interpretation, to explain the connection that exists between the outpouring of the Spirit and Jesus' resurrection:

God has raised this Jesus, and we are all witnesses to it; and now, exalted by God's right hand, he has received from the Father the Holy Spirit, which had been promised, and he has poured out that Spirit; that is what you see and hear (2:32-33).

The bystanders can see for themselves the effects of the Spirit's coming, but they need instruction in order to understand that the Spirit they see poured out upon Jesus' disciples comes to them as a personal gift from Jesus. To be empowered to bestow this gift on them, it was necessary that Jesus go to God, who alone can grant the Spirit. But Jesus could not reach God unless God had brought him forth from the grave and raised him into his own presence. Thus the outpouring of the Spirit upon Jesus' disciples is seen to be a consequence of Jesus' resurrection. The visible and audible manifestation of the Spirit's presence may convince the inhabitants of Jerusalem of the reality of the resurrection itself. The bystanders at Pentecost do not have a direct experience of the resurrection, such as the apostles had when they saw the risen Jesus himself, but they do experience it indirectly, for the phenomena they perceive are visible and audible effects of the resurrection.

Miracles of another kind, the healings, also bear witness to the reality of Jesus' resurrection and heavenly exaltation. Peter explains this clearly after the cure of the lame man at the Beautiful Gate. The witnesses of the healing are naturally filled with wonder and amazement (3:10, 12), but Peter's task is to lead them to conversion:

The God of Abraham, Isaac and Jacob, the God of our fathers, has glorified his Servant Jesus. . . . He has raised him from the dead, as all of us are witnesses. And by faith in his name this man whom you see and know has been restored to health (3:13, 15-16).

It is by the name of Jesus of Nazareth, him whom you crucified and whom God raised from the dead, it is by his name and no other that this man stands before you hale and sound (4:10).

Since the healing was performed in the name of Jesus, it testifies to the miracle-working power of Jesus' name and thus to his supernatural omnipotence. The healing, therefore, is to be considered a proof of the glorious condition to which God raised Jesus at the resurrection and in which he continues to exist. It is inconceivable that a person whose name exercises such astonishingly active power could himself be dead; and not only must he be alive, but he must have been granted a share in the divine prerogatives by God himself.

Instead of merely attributing the miracles to the risen Christ, it is also possible for us to consider them as God's own testimony to Jesus whom he raised from the dead. "The Lord [God] bore witness to the preaching of his grace by performing signs and miracles through their hands" (14:3). The apostles preach that Jesus, raised up by God, received the power to save those who believe in him, and God confirms this message of the apostles by the miracles that accompany their preaching, for those miracles both point back to the initial miracle God wrought on Easter day and at the same time reveal God's power still salvifically active in the Church.

Thus to grasp the meaning of the miracles it is essential to realize their relation to Jesus' resurrection. Luke puts it well: "With great [miracle-working] power the apostles bore witness to the resurrection of the Lord Jesus" (4:33). Miracles reinforce and guarantee the authority of the apostles' affirmation that Jesus is risen. Miracles must also be seen as the continuation into the present of the action by which God raised Jesus up, and as a manifestation of the fullness of power which Jesus received from God at his resurrection. What the witnesses of the early Christian miracles described in Acts saw and heard, the objects of their sense experience, were the effects of Jesus' resurrection, effects which enabled them to grasp, in an indirect but convincing way, the reality of the resurrection itself. The miracle of Easter is continued by the other miracles that follow it, for they all attest the Easter reality: that God intervened to raise Jesus up, and that the risen Jesus now shares God's sovereign power.

To sum up, we may say that conversion involves a turning toward God or the Lord Jesus, but such a turning presupposes an awareness of their existence and an encounter. The Easter miracle makes such an encounter possible, and the miracles that continue the Easter miracle give the possibility of encounter a certain permanence. Each of them is a *locus* in which the apostles' hearers may encounter directly the God who raised Jesus up and the risen Lord himself.

The Action of Grace. The second form of God's intervention to testify personally on behalf of the risen Christ is more necessary and produces a more profound effect than the impression created by miracles. Only God can touch hearts in such a way as to bring about conversions, and he does this by the action of his grace.

Proclaiming Jesus' resurrection to the members of the Sanhedrin, Peter declares:

> God exalted him by his right hand, making him Leader and Savior, to grant Israel through him repentance and remission of sins (5:31).

Thus it is through the risen Christ that God wishes to grant his forgiveness, offering it to those who accept Jesus as Lord. He grants not only pardon, however, but also repentance, which is the normal condition for forgiveness. Both repentance and forgiveness are gifts of God's grace. And since Peter tells us that the bestowal of this grace was the purpose God had in mind when he raised Jesus up and made him Leader and Savior, the gift of repentance appears to be an effect of God's intervention on Easter day, a continuation of the action by which he raised Jesus.

The gift-quality of repentance is also reflected in the astonished remark of the Jerusalem Christians: "So to the Gentiles, too, God has granted repentance leading to life" (11:18). God's gift is eternal life, but also and prior to that the repentance which gives access to life. In this respect repentance is similar to faith, and the relation of both these prior gifts to eternal life is described in similar terms. For example: "All those who were marked out for eternal life embraced the faith" (13:48). Only the predestined can reach eternal life, just as they alone are capable of faith, which opens their way to eternal life by giving assurance of forgiveness and justification (vv. 37-39). If they embrace the faith, it is because God gives them the gift of faith. This is the same God who gives pagans the faith which cleanses their hearts (15:9), in this way choosing "from among the Gentiles a people for his name" (15:14). Since salvation is a gift of God's free grace, conversion, which opens the path of salvation to us, must be a gift of God as well.

This theology of grace is given very concrete expression in the story of the conversion of Lydia at Philippi. On the level of the external action Paul preaches the Gospel message and Lydia becomes convinced of its truth. But Luke explains what has happened on the level of the deeper causality involved: "The Lord opened her heart, so that she clung to Paul's words" (16:14).

Miracles are not a necessary requirement before a person can accept the Good News of the resurrection. And even where miracles are present, they are never sufficient of themselves without the action of grace, which alone can open hearts. Conversion supposes an encounter with God, toward whom one "turns," and this requires that God reveal himself in action—not just by his past action in raising Jesus from the dead, but by his present action here and now for the sinner in need of conversion. The Easter miracle continues permanently in the Church, and is sometimes experienced in extraordinary visible phenomena but more frequently in the secret, sovereign action of God's grace in human hearts.

The Resurrection: A Past Event
Decisive for the Future

Jesus' resurrection is an event of the past. It is also the harbinger of a future event, for it should remind us that we stand under the threat of the final judgment. The peroration of Paul's speech in Athens is especially clear in this regard:

> God now makes known to all men everywhere that they must repent, because he has set a day on which to judge the universe with justice by a man whom he has appointed, and he has given all a guarantee of that by raising that man from the dead (17:30-31).

God has already set the day for the general judgment and appointed the one who is to preside at the supreme tribunal. Notice of these momentous decisions was served when God raised Jesus from the dead, for Jesus' resurrection is the guarantee God gives to convince men of Jesus' appointment as sovereign Judge and also to warn them that from now on he may have to exercise his function at any time. Thus the resurrection of Jesus places the human race in a new situation. The consequence of this new situation is clearly that men must repent, and Paul explicitates the reason: men are to repent *because* judgment may occur at any moment.

The total picture may become clearer if we add one final consideration and describe the full process in this way: the prospect of judgment ought to induce men to repent so that they may obtain the forgiveness of their sins which leads to eternal life. This fuller picture is suggested by the final remarks of Peter's speech at Caesarea:

> After he rose from the dead, he ordered us to preach to the people and to testify that he is the one God has appointed to judge the living and the dead. To him all the prophets bear witness, that whoever believes in him will receive, through his name, the forgiveness of his sins (10:42-43).

The announcement of judgment has a definite place in the preaching, for the prospect of having to give an account of their sins will fill men with fear. But at the same time they are assured that the sovereign Judge offers forgiveness to all who believe in him. Hence the necessity of faith. And the compelling motive for faith, in turn, is precisely the judgment that is predicted: a person must believe in order to obtain pardon for his sins and thus be ready for the judgment when it comes. Thus the very thought of judgment can lead to conversion. Even as a motive for conversion, however, the judgment cannot be conceived apart from the resurrection of Jesus, since it is precisely Jesus' resurrection which guarantees the announcement of the coming judgment.

To be saved on the day of judgment, therefore, we must believe, or, as Joel puts it, we must "call on the name of the Lord" (Joel 3:5; cf. Acts 2:21). If we acknowledge Jesus as Lord, we have hope of escaping the catastrophe that threatens sinners, and for that reason Peter urges: "Save yourselves from this perverse generation!" (2:40). Salvation depends on the name of the Lord Jesus, in whom we must have faith: "There is no other name under heaven given to men by which we are to be saved" (4:12). Consequently, refusal to believe amounts to self-exclusion from eternal life, as Paul intimates when he tells the Jews of Antioch in Pisidia: "You reject God's word and deem yourselves unworthy of eternal life" (13:46). Finally, in response to the question of his jailor at Philippi "What must I do to be saved?" Paul responds: "Believe in the Lord Jesus and you shall be saved, and your household with you" (16:30-31). Thus faith is at once the pledge of the forgiveness of our sins and also our assurance of salvation on the day of judgment.

In his discourse at the Beautiful Gate, Peter envisages the end of time from a particular point of view. He considers conversion here not as a means of assuring one's personal salvation on judgment day, but as a way of hastening the time of salvation, which will coincide with the glorious return of Jesus.

> Repent and be converted, so that your sins may be blotted out and the Lord may send the time of refreshment: that he may send the Christ who has been destined for you, Jesus, whom heaven must hold until the time of universal restoration, of which God has spoken by the mouth of the holy prophets (3:19-21).

This text gives prominence to the idea that the parousia is to inaugurate an era of happiness. But this cannot happen until men are ready for it, and hence the thought of hastening the coming of those blessed times should impel men to conversion.

Because of the close connection between Jesus' resurrection and the events of the end-time which we have been considering, the preaching of the resurrection necessarily involves a threat for unconverted sinners, the threat of the terrible judgment that will divide men into the elect and the rejected. But to those who believe and are converted the message of the resurrection offers a firm hope of salvation. In those who accept the message, faith generates hope, and begets also that distinctive joy and happiness characteristic of new converts. Recall the example of the jailor at Philippi who "rejoiced with his whole household at his new-found faith in God" (16:34), and of the Ethiopian eunuch who had just received baptism and who "continued his journey filled with joy" (8:39). Remember also the Samaritans, at whose conversion "there was great joy in the city" (8:8), and the converts at Antioch in Pisidia and at Derbe who "rejoiced and glorified the word of the Lord," like the disciples themselves who "were filled with joy and with the Holy Spirit" (13:48, 52). In all of these passages there reappears the same mood that characterized the gatherings of the Church from the beginning, when the first Christians in Jerusalem used to "take their food in joy and simplicity of heart" (2:46).

Thus the resurrection of Jesus, as sign and anticipation of the end-time, invites sinners to return into themselves, to repent, and to believe, so as to obtain forgiveness of their sins before the final judgment. Those who are already converted, on the other hand, who believe in the Lord Jesus, find in his resurrection a motive for hope and joyful trust, confident that Jesus, at his return, will be their Savior and will grant them a share in the inheritance with all the saints (cf. 20:32).

III. CHANGE OF LIFE

Up to this point we have been satisfied to deal with the verb *epistrephein* in its etymological sense of *turning toward*, and we have emphasized that conversion consists in turning toward a person, God or the Lord Jesus, in response to an action that reveals that person's presence: when God raises Jesus up, Jesus leaves the grave behind and takes his seat at the right hand of God. It is now time to point out that the translation we have been using is not entirely accurate. "Being converted" is not only a "turning toward" God or the Lord Jesus, but also a "coming back." When the Greek verb *epistrephein* is used, it is not merely a question of facing in a new direction while remaining in the same place; the verb supposes both a change of direction and a movement. The image is that of a man retracing his steps: a person who was walking away from God has changed direction and is now coming back to him. This meaning of the verb is found in secular Greek usage as well, but it is quite frequent and common in biblical Greek, owing to the influence of the Hebrew verb *shub.* A convert's change of stance in relation to God means in practice a reorientation in his whole way of life, complete transformation of his conduct. Turning toward God means setting out on the road that leads to him.

Returning to God

There is also a negative side to conversion, for it involves giving up evil deeds. Peter's speech at the Beautiful Gate contains an appeal to the people of Jerusalem, an appeal which is restated in another form at the conclusion of the speech:

Repent and be converted, so that your sins may be blotted out (3:19).

It is for your sake first of all that God raised up his Servant, and he has sent him to bless you, provided each of you turn away from his iniquities (3:26).

The first of these appeals is worded in the form of an invitation to conversion, the second as an invitation to turn away from evil. The two verses contain a word play on two Greek verbs (*epistrephein* and *apostrephein* = "to turn toward" and "to turn away"), and the antithesis is certainly deliberate. This pointed contrast is still evident in the text even if we read verse 26, as some prefer to read it, more as a promise that Christ will turn us around than as an exhortation to turn ourselves from our iniquities. In either case, however, conversion evidently implies giving up evil deeds. We have already seen that pagans, in turning toward the true God, had to turn away from idols; and now Peter, speaking here to Jews, explains that the conversion expected of them obliges them to turn away from sin.

The positive side of the change produced in the convert appears in Paul's summary of his preaching before King Agrippa:

First to the inhabitants of Damascus, next to those of Jerusalem and the whole land of Judea, and then to the pagans, I declared that they should repent and turn back [be converted] to God by doing works befitting repentance (26:20).

After urging his audience to repent of their past misdeeds, Paul requires of them for the future a pattern of behavior appropriate to their repentance, and he specifies that conversion concretely consists in the practice of righteous deeds. John the Baptist expressed the same idea metaphorically in his appeal: "Bring forth fruit worthy of repentance" (Luke 3:8). Authentic conversion is recognized by its fruits; it is concretized in the actions it inspires. For this reason a convert must not only deplore his own conduct in the past, he must also behave henceforward in a wholly new way.

On another occasion, speaking before a pagan audience at Lystra, Paul remarks that, though "in past generations God let all nations follow their own ways," the time has now come for them to "be converted to the true God, who made heaven and earth and the sea and whatever is in them" (14:15-16). Conversion obviously implies that the pagans must give up their own ways so as to follow other ways that God will show them. They must renounce idol worship, to adore only the true God. Further, they can no longer go on living, as they did while still pagans, in a manner incompatible with the holiness that God requires of his servants.

Between "turning around" (*retournement*) and "coming back" (*retour*) there is quite a difference. Turning around takes only an instant. Coming back involves a long journey. Consequently, any conversion, even the most sincere, entails a demand for fidelity and perseverance. The preaching of the first missionaries at Antioch produced fine results: "Great was the number of those who embraced the faith and were converted to the Lord" (11:21). But the story did not end there. For when Barnabas arrived in the city, even though he was delighted at the results he witnessed, yet he also took thought for the future and "exhorted all of them to remain faithful to the Lord with a steadfast heart" (v. 23). Once converted, we must persevere (*prosmenein*) on the path which we have begun to walk.

The "Way"

The convert adopts a new way of life. The question immediately arises: What will the rule and norms of his conduct be from now on?

In the opinion of some, the so-called "Judaizers," the norm of behavior in Christianity must remain the same as it was in Judaism, namely the Law of Moses. They argue that "if you do not let yourself be circumcised in the manner that comes from Moses, you cannot be saved," and that therefore "the pagans should be circumcised and commanded to observe the Law of Moses" (15:1, 5). But this point of view is eventually rejected, and another prevails, namely:

> It is not necessary to burden those among the pagans who are converted to God. ... We should not try to impose upon the disciples a yoke which neither our fathers nor we ourselves were able to bear (15:19, 10).

From now on the Christian way of life will be different from life in Israel; Christians will no longer be subject to the Mosaic Law.

To help us define the Christian rule of life, it will be useful to focus our attention on one particular term from the vocabulary of Acts: the "way." The image of the path or road is quite in harmony with the image suggested by the term "conversion": the convert is one who comes back to God, and the rule which he follows for this return is the road, the way which God shows him.

An excellent starting point for a consideration of the theme of the way in Acts is Paul's speech before the governor Felix. Tertullus, spokesman for the high priest, has accused Paul of being one of the leaders of the Nazarean "sect" (24:5). But Paul takes exception to that term and substitutes a word more to his own liking in his reply:

> I admit it openly. It is according to the way, which they call a "sect," that I serve the God of my fathers (v. 14).

The way is the Christian manner of serving God, of rendering him the worship due him. The underlying image survives in this usage, for in biblical and Semitic language the word denotes a way of living, of behaving—that is, of "walking." Paul claims that he continues to serve the God of Israel, even though he has taken up the Christian way of life.

This way of life is so distinctive that Christianity itself comes to be called the way, and Christians become known as "followers of the way," or more literally "those who belong to the way" (9:2). We hear of calumnies against the way (19:9), of a riot provoked by reaction to the way (19:23), and of persecutions directed against the way (22:4). This way is the Christian concept of a life that is religious and pleasing to God; it is also the Christian community itself, considered from the viewpoint of its characteristic life-style. The expression always implies a relation to God: it is God's way. It is the mode of conduct that God proposes to those who wish to serve him and "return" to him. Jewish theology identifies God's way with the Law, the supreme norm in accordance with which each Israelite is to model his life. Early Christianity, on the contrary, believed that the way of life practiced in the community was itself the concrete embodiment of God's way.

A definition of the way would amount to a definition of Christian morality, that is, of the patterns of behavior by which Christians endeavor to render service to God. Certain traits stand out, of course, as more typical. The most obvious example would be what Acts calls *koinonia*, or fraternal communion, which involves both unanimity of spirit and also a sharing of temporal goods with those in need (cf. 2:44; 4:32). This is the community spirit of those who know that they are all members of a single family. Christians are known by the love they have for one another. In a wider sense they can also be recognized by the striving for holiness that marks their lives and that sets them apart both from pagans, who are not so preoccupied with sanctity, and from the Jews, who conceive it too ritualistically.

In the second part of this study we emphasized that conversion is adherence to a person, to God who raised Jesus up, and to the Lord Jesus himself. We also stressed the element of personal encounter in conversion, which brings the individual face to face with God. In this third section we have been attempting to fill in details that will complete the picture. There was nothing individualistic about the early Christian notion of conversion. The return to God which is the essence of conversion can only be accomplished by following the path that God himself has marked out, and concretely this path is identical with the life-style characteristic of the Christian community. We may even go so far as to say that it is identical with this community itself. The convert becomes a member of the community not only by an initial act of entrance, his baptism, but by a whole lifetime thereafter lived in conformity with the community's understanding about how God should be served. He enters a living community and has to assimilate himself to it by his entire behavior. It is within that community, and profoundly integrated into it by his life-style, that he achieves his "return" to God. The community provides him with the living norm that will be for him the way of God. The new life into which he enters is essentially ecclesial.

CONCLUSION

The Acts of the Apostles enables us to form a fairly complete idea of how the early Christians understood conversion. Although their notion undoubtedly owes much to Jewish tradition, yet it has been completely rethought in the light of the Christian message.

A. The Jews vehemently reproached the pagans for the sinfulness of their idol-worship. The apostles, in turn, tried to make the Jews of Jerusalem conscious of the sin they had committed in crucifying Jesus. A prerequisite for conversion in every case is that an individual or a group become aware of having sinned against God.

B. Jewish missionaries urged pagans to renounce their vain idols and turn toward the living God, the Creator of the universe. The apostles call both Jews and Gentiles to turn to the living God who revealed himself by raising Jesus from the dead. Whoever acknowledges God's action in the Easter event must acknowledge the risen Jesus as Lord.

C. The Jews were waiting for a visible and dazzling intervention by God that would put an end to the present age, annihilate or subdue the Gentile nations, and bring unprecedented happiness to the chosen people. Christians wait for the eschatological intervention with even greater impatience because they are convinced that Jesus' resurrection was already a preparation for this intervention. The one who is to carry out the last judgment is already empowered for his function, and this view of things provides a motive for conversion. All men, pagans as well as Jews, are invited to get ready for the judgment by being converted and by accepting the lordship of Jesus in faith. In this way they will obtain a share in the happiness of the coming age.

D. In Jewish opinion, pagans could not obtain salvation simply by coming to believe that God was one and unique; they would also have to observe the Law of Moses, the charter of God's Covenant with his people. Nor would the early Christians have considered a conversion authentic if the convert in question accepted the Gospel message but did not also embrace the life-style of the apostolic community. A new Christian has to become a member of the community and to identify with its distinctive way of serving God.

Community of Goods
in the Early Church

The Pentecost narrative in the Acts of the Apostles gives us a vivid account of Peter's first preaching to Jewish crowds and of the enthusiastic reception of his message by many of those who heard him. The success of Peter's speech is striking indeed: about three thousand persons accepted his invitation to baptism and were added that day to the Christian community. Luke then brings his treatment of Pentecost to a close by a summary sketch of the common life of those new converts, starting with this observation:

> They devoted themselves to the apostles' teaching, to the *koinonia*, to the breaking of the bread and the prayers (Acts 2:42).

Most of the terms in this description are quite clear and cause no serious difficulty to interpreters. But the word *koinonia*, which we have left untranslated, is ambiguous and requires further definition. In the present essay we shall focus our attention on that term and some related expressions in Acts, in the hope that closer analysis of Luke's language may shed greater light on the picture of the early Christian community he wished to draw for us.

The standard lexicon of Bauer-Arndt-Gingrich distinguishes four meanings of the Greek word *koinonia* in the New Testament. The word may designate: (1) association, communion, fellowship, close relationship with persons or things; (2) generosity, fellow-feeling, altruism, that is, the sense one has of community with others and of the obligations which flow from that community; (3) concrete manifestations of this sense of community: a proof of brotherly unity, or even a gift or contribution; (4) finally, participation, sharing in something that affects others, such as their feelings, their actions, and their sufferings.

85

A variety of interpretations may be found for the use of the term *koinonia* in Acts 2:42, cited above. For example, Lake and Cadbury mention four distinct possibilities here. The word might apply to (1) the union of the faithful with the apostles or (2) the practice of community of goods. (3) The word could also be equivalent to the expression "the breaking of the bread," so that the third expression in verse 42 would be in apposition to the second and would explain it. (4) Finally the word might be another way of referring to almsgiving. Menoud gives another classification of the possibilities, stating that *koinonia* in this verse may refer to (1) the spiritual communion that unites believers with each other and with the apostles, (2) the material communion brought about by sharing of temporal goods, (3) the eucharistic communion which unites the faithful with Christ by means of the sacrament, or (4) the ecclesiastical communion, the unity of the faithful manifested by the collection.

Jeremias believes that we can detect in the four terms employed in Acts 2:42 allusions to four successive phases in a Christian liturgy. In earlier studies Jeremias identified the *koinonia* with the collection of goods destined for the "daily distribution," the relief service mentioned in Acts 6:1, but more recently he prefers to identify it with the table-fellowship realized by the common meal, the "agape," to which the eucharistic rite of the "breaking of the bread" belonged. Reicke also favors a liturgical interpretation of the term. He rejects a "centripetal" understanding, such as the notion of a communion produced by sharing in a common good, in favor of a "centrifugal" understanding: the first Christians entered enthusiastically into the distribution of goods that took place during the liturgical gatherings.

This rapid survey of opinions will be sufficient to help us realize the variety of interpretations proposed for the word *koinonia*; no consensus has yet been reached about its meaning in Acts 2:42. Our own working hypothesis, however, is that Luke, who is responsible for verse 42 in its present shape and wording, has himself explained what he means by the *koinonia* of the early Christians. He gives us the further specifics we need to fill out and grasp his understanding of Christian fellowship especially in two other passages from the opening chapters of Acts, both quite similar in character and vocabulary to the verse which served as our starting point. The first of these passages comes almost immediately after Acts 2:42:

> All the believers held everything together in common (*hapanta koina*); they would sell their properties and possessions and distribute the proceeds among all, to each one according to his needs (Acts 2:44-45).

The same idea recurs several chapters later, once more in a general summary typifying the nature of early Christian community life:

> The multitude of those who had come to the faith was a single heart and soul, and no one called any of his possessions his own, but among them everything was common (*panta koina*). As a result nobody was in need among them, for all those who owned lands or houses would sell them, and bring the sale price and lay it at the feet of the apostles; distribution was then made to each one according to his needs (Acts 4:32, 34-35).

These later remarks make it quite clear that Luke understood the *koinonia* of the first Christians as a reference first of all to their practice of sharing their possessions. Their fellowship, however, does not seem to be limited to the level of material goods, but appears to imply a more spiritual communion as well. Let us look more closely at each of these aspects in turn.

I. COMMUNITY OF GOODS

Among Them Everything Was Common

The similarity of the expressions, "they held everything in common" (2:44) and "among them everything was common" (4:32), catches our attention immediately, and the adjective "common" (*koina*), used in both of these verses, obviously echoes the statement about *koinonia* in 2:42. The affirmation that "among them everything was common" in 4:32 simply repeats in a positive form what has just been stated negatively in the preceding phrase, "no one called any of his possessions his own" (*elegon idion einai*); the two parts of this verse shed mutual light upon one another.

Now exegetes have known for a long time that these phrases and formulas from the Acts of the Apostles would have been extremely suggestive to Greek ears. Moreover, Luke must have been quite aware of the strong associations his language would carry and the precise memories it would awaken in the readers for whom he was writing. The themes alluded to in the expressions which Luke employs are so rich and dense, in fact, that we will probably find it helpful at the outset to distinguish three main currents in them:

A. There is first of all what we might call the theme of "the Golden Age." At the very beginning, private property was unknown. Authors lavish loving descriptions on that period of primitive happiness when everything was owned in common by all, and they still look back to those simpler times for the ideal of a social life consonant with nature. This theme is especially dear to the Pythagoreans, who report that Pythagoras and his disciples practiced this ideal form of community, just as it had been in the beginning. The theme fascinated Plato, who represents the beginnings of Athens according to this pattern, and who also models upon it his *Republic*, a utopia in which complete communism would be practiced. Aristophanes made fun of this utopia, and Aristotle retained only such details from Plato's ideal state as were reconcilable with his own realistic common sense. Yet these theories about the ideal human condition in harmony with nature continued to win adherents in the later Cynic, Stoic and Neo-Pythagorean schools.

All this familiar data should not lead us, however, to the rash conclusion that Luke, desirous of presenting the beginnings of the Church as the Golden Age of Christianity, was content merely to evoke in this connection the myth of the ideal origins of mankind. There is additional, more precise evidence that deserves to be taken into consideration as well, and that will contribute to a fuller picture of Luke's intention.

B. At various times and places, practical and concrete experiments in common ownership were undertaken. The community of goods practiced by the Pythagoreans was, of course, influenced by their philosophical theories, but such theories probably had no influence at all on the various attempts at "communism" of which history preserves the memory, such as those in the Lipari Islands, in Crete, and in Sparta. Nor was the community of goods practiced by the Essenes in Palestine based on Greek theories about the original Golden Age or the natural human condition. It is all the more surprising, therefore, to hear Flavius Josephus explaining to his Greek and Roman readers that "the Essene sect practices the manner of life that Pythagoras taught the Greeks" (*Antiquities* XV:371). He goes even further and presents the Essene way of life in such terms as to make it appear like the realization of a philosophical, more specifically a Stoic, ideal:

They scorn wealth, and their community life (*to koinonikon*) is a marvel. You would look in vain among them for any individual richer than the others, for it is a rule that those who enter the sect give their wealth over to the order. Consequently you do not find among them either the lowliness produced by indigence, or the pride that comes of wealth. Rather each one's possessions are pooled with those of others, so that there exists among them only one common ownership, as with brothers (*The Jewish War* II:122).

Elsewhere he comments:

Their goods are held in common, and the wealthy individual reaps no more benefit from his property than the one who owns absolutely nothing (*Antiquities* XVIII:20).

Since Luke had Greek readers in mind while writing, just as Josephus did, it should not surprise us that he described the life of the first Christians in language that would remind his readers of an ideal both familiar and attractive to them. The use of such a literary device does not imply by any means that the community of goods Luke attributed to the first Christians was a pure figment of his imagination.

C. "Among friends, everything is common" (*koina ta philon*). This maxim expresses both the precise form that sharing of possessions generally takes and the concrete context in which the ideal is practiced. Timaeus of Tauromenium, as quoted by Diogenes Laertius, tells us that the maxim goes back to Pythagoras, and that the way of life practiced by the Pythagoreans was simply the practical implementation of the maxim:

According to Timaeus, Pythagoras was the first to say, "Friends have all things in common" (*koina ta philon*) and "Friendship is equality" (*philia isotes*). And in fact his disciples did put all their possessions together into one common stock (*Life of Pythagoras* VIII:10).

Whether or not the slogan came originally from Pythagoras, it was widely known and quite often quoted as early as the fifth century. Plato liked to refer to it. Aristotle recorded his agreement with this saying, and compared it with other proverbs that speak of friendship:

> "Among friends everything is common" is quite correct, for friendship consists in sharing (*koinonia*) (*Nicomachean Ethics* VIII:11; 1159 B, 31).

> All the maxims agree, for example "one soul" and "among friends everything is common" and "friendship is equality" (IX:8; 1168 B, 8).

Euripides quoted the saying directly several times, and also seems to have paraphrased it in the following verses:

> True friends cling not to private property;
> Their wealth is shared in close community (*Andromache* 376f.).

Menander quoted it in his *Brothers*, and so did Terence. Plutarch records it as part of a citation from Theophrastus, and Athenaeus mentions it among the sayings of Cratinus. The maxim is also found among the Latins, in Martial, Cicero and Seneca, to mention only a few examples.

It is evident that community of goods as practiced among friends is not a juridical arrangement. It is not as if each party made a legal renunciation of goods in order to set up a common fund to be shared with his friend or friends. The idea is simply that affection for his friends would move a person to put all his goods at their disposal, without wanting to keep anything back for himself alone. When a friend is in need, we do not hesitate to give him all the help possible. The friendship we feel for him makes us consider the goods at our disposal as common resources.

This way of looking at things surely sheds a good deal of light on our subject, at least on the statement of Acts 4:32 that "no one called any of his possessions his own, but among them everything was common." There is no question in this case of legal transfer of titles, for each individual remains owner of his possessions, but affection for his brothers impels each one to put what he has at their disposal. Such an attitude goes far beyond a mere charitable inclination to generosity and almsgiving, for in the case we are considering the legitimate owner will consider his goods a common patrimony and himself merely their administrator; his brothers in need may ask him for what they require as if it belonged to them. The same interpretation easily applies as well to the expression in Acts 2:44 that "they held everything in common"; there is no necessary connotation of legal ownership in the verb Luke uses there.

Other evidence provided by Acts still remains to be examined before our study of community of goods will be complete. The reader can probably already recall other passages that favor the same non-juridical exegesis we have been proposing. For example, when we read that the first Christians were "a single heart and soul" (4:32), we naturally think of the proverb "one soul" which Aristotle associated with the maxim "Among friends, all is common." We will have occasion to consider this complex of ideas later on in the second section of this chapter. But on the other hand, when we read about believers who sell their possessions in order to pool the proceeds, that statement obviously suggests to us more than a mere moral community of goods inspired by mutual affection. And in trying to fill in the details of a total picture, we must also take into account the evidence of such texts as that.

Nobody Was in Need among Them

Once we have discovered that the *koinonia* of which Acts speaks has literary antecedents in Hellenism, we might be tempted to search in the same direction for the roots of the expression, "nobody was in want among them" (4:34). And promising leads would not be difficult to find. We may recall, for instance, Seneca's remarks about the primitive period when common ownership was practiced:

> What men were ever happier than they? They enjoyed the world in common. ... Oh, the unparalleled wealth of that race of men, in which you could not find a single pauper (*Letter* 90:38).

Yet interesting as such parallels may be in themselves, the precise form which Luke gives to his expression in Acts 4:34 encourages us rather to look for influences from another quarter than Hellenism.

Commentators judge—and they are surely correct in this—that Luke's expression is an echo of the Old Testament, and specifically of Deuteronomy 15:4. The original Hebrew text of this verse contains a recommendation. After speaking of the concern which should be had for the underprivileged, the legislator adds: "Yet, let there be nobody in need among you, because the Lord your God will bless you ... only if you listen to his voice." The Greek translation, the Septuagint, employs a future tense in the opening clause: "There will be nobody in need among you, because the Lord your God will bless you ... if you listen to his voice." Since this Greek sentence is quite long and the conditional clause, "if you listen to his voice," comes only after a lengthly reference to the divine blessing, the first part of the sentence might tend to be interpreted as a promise rather than a recommendation. And this is in fact the way the Targum understands it: "If you carry out the precepts of the Law, no one will be needy among you, because Yahweh will bless you. ..." (*Targ. Jer.* I).

In its Jewish context this promise naturally acquires eschatological overtones: in the final times all Israelites will be faithful to the Law, and there will no longer be any person in need among them. Christians, conscious as they were of being the messianic community of the final times, must have begun quite early to apply this promise to themselves. Thus the fact of having nobody in want in the Christian community would take on the value of a sign. Since Moses' promise has been fulfilled among them, they are the promised messianic community become a present reality.

Finally it should be mentioned, however, that Luke does not explicitly cite the passage from Deuteronomy to which his text seems to allude, and that no detail in the immediate context of Acts 4:34 holds up the early Christian behavior in question as the fulfillment of a prophecy. Hence, though we are justified in supposing that the formula, "nobody was in want among them," really echoes the wording of Deuteronomy, it would seem likely that the text of Deuteronomy influenced the Christian tradition at some stage prior to Luke's own composition, and that Luke himself is directly dependent only on that earlier tradition. In that case, one could also easily imagine that Luke, on finding the expression "nobody was in want among them" in his source, might not have recalled Deuteronomy at all, but might have been reminded spontaneously of more or less parallel themes then fashionable in the Hellenistic world.

They Would Sell Their Properties

Two short texts furnish further details about the practice of community of goods among the first Christians:

> They would sell their properties and possessions and distribute the proceeds among all, to each one according to his need (2:45).

> All those who owned lands or houses would sell them, and bring the sale price and lay it at the feet of the apostles; distribution was then made to each one according to his needs (4:34-35).

A. Immediately after the second of these texts, Luke calls attention to the generosity of Barnabas: "Since he possessed a field, he sold it, brought the money and laid it at the feet of the apostles" (4:37). We are surprised to hear Luke repeating almost verbatim in this verse what he has just said in the previous one, and even more surprised to hear Barnabas praised individually for something which all have just been described as doing. The story of Barnabas is followed by the much less exemplary case history of Ananias and Saphira (5:1-11). This couple likewise sells a piece of property, but the husband puts aside part of the price and brings only the difference to lay at the feet of the apostles. Peter reproaches Ananias for his behavior. It is important, however, to pay close attention to the specifics of this reproach. Peter does not blame him for keeping something back; clearly he was free to hold on to his property if he wished, and free also, once he had sold it, to dispose of the proceeds as he pleased. What Ananias is reproached for is his attempt at deception: he wanted to deceive the apostles by letting them believe that he was bringing them the entire price from the sale. The evidence is clear here that Christians were not compelled or obliged to divest themselves of their possessions for the benefit of the community. Thus Luke's praise of Barnabas in Acts 4:36-37 has real meaning, for such an act of generosity must have been exceptional.

In the light of these facts, which Luke probably derives from early traditions, the rather global assertions of Acts 2:45 and 4:34-35 should be reduced to their proper proportions. Doubtless they are generalizations, though based on specific cases. However it is a common literary device to attribute to all the conduct of a few, and we should not mistake the nature or intention of such a generalization. What Luke clearly wants to call to our attention is the marvelous example of those early Christians, however few or many they may have been, who pushed generosity to its furthest limits. The same concern on Luke's part to stress the detachment of the first Christians and to hold it up as an example for the Church of his own day was an obvious motive force in the composition of his Gospel as well (cf. Luke 5:11, 18; 14:33; 18:22).

B. Other information supplied in Acts also encourages us to take seriously the generosity of the first Christians. Acts 6:1ff. informs us that a "daily distribution" had been organized quite early within the community, especially on behalf of widows, and that reorganization of this relief service, and therefore of the community itself, was soon required in order to reduce friction between the "Hebrews" and the "Hellenists." A service such as that amounted to the kind of burden that could be carried only by generous and unselfish charity. As a matter of fact, the Jerusalem community soon fell into need and was forced to appeal to the other churches for help. We know this from Acts (cf. 11:29-30), but also from Paul, who was greatly preoccupied during his third missionary journey by his collection on behalf of the poor in Jerusalem (cf. Galatians 2:10; 1 Corinthians 16:1-3; 2 Corinthians 8—9; Romans 15:25-28). It is easy to understand the eventual distress of the mother Church when we remember acts of generosity such as that attributed to Barnabas. Though Luke has undoubtedly generalized in saying that all sold their goods to create a common fund, yet it would not be difficult to explain the impoverishment of the whole community as a result of numerous instances of generous giving.

C. A final remark may be in order concerning the spirit that inspired these acts of generosity, as Luke depicts the situation for us. On two occasions Luke enunciates the principle: "to each one according to his needs" (Acts 2:45; 4:35). The point is that everyone should have what is necessary; in practice, Christians are to see to it "that there be no one in need among them." The ideal they strive for is not precisely voluntary detachment and poverty, but rather the ideal of a charity which cannot tolerate need among one's own. Christians did not give up their possessions out of a desire to be poor, but out of a desire to eliminate poverty among their brethren, so that there would no longer be any poor among them.

The detachment thus revealed is only a natural consequence of the very deep sense of solidarity that should unite fellow Christians with one another. We shall see shortly that this ideal corresponds quite closely with the Pauline ideal of the "equality" that ought to exist among Christians. Equality, which Hellenism considered the specific trait of friendship, was also to be the distinctive mark of brotherly love among Christians. Thus to understand accurately the ideal that Luke portrays in Acts, we must realize clearly that the sharing of material goods is but the manifestation of a deeper, spiritual communion. To this aspect of the subject we now turn.

II. COMMUNION OF SOULS

Adequate consideration of the subject of community of goods in the summaries in Acts must also take into account the opening statement of Acts 4:32:

> The multitude of those who had come to the faith was a single heart and soul (*kardia kai psyche mia*). . . .

This opening affirmation is inseparable from the remainder of the verse:

> . . . and no one called any of his possessions his own, but among them everything was common.

The two parts of this verse constitute a single sentence, and they deal with two features of early Christian community life which appear intrinsically interconnected. Our initial impression is that the two features mentioned in this verse are complementary to one another, and that the latter may be a natural consequence of the former. In that case, it is the spiritual unity existing among Christians which leads to their sharing material goods. We desire in the present section to demonstrate that that initial impression is solidly grounded. We will show that the opening of verse 32 sheds light on Luke's understanding of community of goods in the early Church. We must begin by examining the characteristic language Luke employs in that verse.

A Single Soul

A. Luke writes that the community of believers was "a single heart and soul." The juxtaposition of "heart" and "soul" in this formula is quite unparalleled in Hellenism, yet quite typical in the Bible. Recall, for instance, the well-known commandment to love God "with one's whole heart and one's whole soul" (cf. Deuteronomy 4:29 and *passim*), or the invitation to put God's words "into one's heart and into one's soul" (6:6; 11:18). The context of these expressions in Deuteronomy, however, has scarcely any connection with the idea of unanimity, which is the point Luke emphasizes. We come closer to Luke's idea in 1 Chronicles 12:39 where we are told that the people is "of one heart" to make David king. For the Hebrew expression "one heart" (*leb 'ehad*) the Greek translator writes "one soul" (*psyche mia*), as if he felt that the expression "one soul" would better express the notion of unanimity in Greek. We may well wonder whether "one soul" is not the expression that would spontaneously have come to Luke's mind, and whether he may have added the word "heart" in this context (he likes to use it elsewhere as well) to form the familiar double formula and give his text a more biblical sound. At any rate, it is the expression "one soul" that is really characteristic in Acts 4:32.

B. We have already encountered the passage in which Aristotle suggests the essence of friendship by quoting three maxims, "one soul," "among friends all is common," and "friendship is equality." Diogenes Laertius (V:20) tells us that when Aristotle was asked what a friend is, he answered: "one soul dwelling in two bodies." Euripides alludes to the same proverb when Electra tells Orestes that she is his sister, forming only "a single soul" with him (*Orestes* 1046). Plutarch spells out the meaning more fully:

He who is taken over and inspired by Eros starts by eliminating the expressions "mine" and "not mine," just as Plato excluded them from his ideal republic, for we can say quite simply that friends possess everything in common (*koina ta philon*). This is true, however, only of those who, though existing in separate bodies, actively unite and fuse their souls together, no longer wishing or considering themselves to be two separate beings (*The Dialogue on Love* 21:9; 967 E).

Cicero alludes to the same proverb several times in his treatise on friendship:

The essence of friendship lies in (the formation of) a single soul, as it were, from several (*On Friendship* 25:92).

[A man] searches for another, whose soul will so merge with his own as to form one, as it were, where there had been two (21:81).

Cicero also refers in a similar context to the famous saying of Pythagoras:

When two people are united by the same interests and desires, each of them can come to love the other as himself, and then Pythagoras' requirement for ideal friendship is achieved, namely that two become one (*De Officiis* I:17,56).

On the basis of such passages as these, we are of the opinion that the expression "one soul," when encountered in a context which also recalls the theme "among friends all is common," would spontaneously have reminded Luke's original readers of the notion of friendship which was prevalent at that time in the Greco-Roman world.

C. Paul employs the expression "one soul" in an exhortation to the Christian community at Philippi:

Be steadfast in one spirit, struggling together with one soul for the faith of the Gospel (Philippians 1:27).

He continues this exhortation a few verses later, with a variety of synonyms that clarify and explain the meaning of the expression which concerns us:

Fill up my joy by being of the same mind, having the same love, being united in soul and of one mind (2:2).

Notice that in the first of these texts "one soul" is preceded by a reference to "one spirit." When the soul is mentioned in Jewish writings it is frequently accompanied by synonymous expressions, as we have seen illustrated by several passages from Deuteronomy which couple "heart" and "soul" and also by a similar duplication of expressions in Acts 4:32. From the two texts from Philippians cited above, we may conclude that for several individuals or a group to constitute "a single soul" (*mia psyche*) is identical with being "united in soul" (*sympsychoi*) and also with "being of one or the same mind" (*to hen/auto phronein*). By this variety of formulas Paul expresses the concord and unanimity (literally: "one-soulness") which he wishes to see growing stronger among the Christians at Philippi.

A later chapter of the letter to the Philippians contains an appeal addressed to two individuals to "be of one mind," that is, to live in harmony. The same expression recurs in 2 Corinthians 13:11 and, in a slightly different form, in Romans 12:16 and 15:5. A similar exhortation is found in the First Letter of Peter:

> Be all of one mind (*homophrones*), united in brotherly love and sympathy and compassion for one another (3:8).

Such examples of early Christian parenesis all shed light on Luke's thought and intention when he describes the first Christians as constituting "one heart and soul." What Luke desires to emphasize is the perfect concord, the total spiritual union which prevails among them.

These non-Lucan texts reveal concerns quite similar to those which must have motivated Luke to speak of the unanimity of the first Christians. Does the language of these texts also confirm our earlier observations about the literary roots of the expression "one soul" in Acts? In general, yes. The characteristic formula in the Pauline texts we have cited, the expression "to be of one mind," is not biblical, but it is found with some frequency in Hellenistic literature. Thus Paul's passages would seem to support our hypothesis that we should look to a Hellenistic literary milieu in general for the origin of Luke's expression "one soul." But the expression "to be of one mind" is used in Hellenism in a rather wide sense to refer to people who are of the same opinion, who share identical sentiments and have a common purpose, or who live together in harmony. Sometimes the expression is found, to be sure, in treatments of the theme of friendship, but not frequently, and there is no evidence of a specific relationship between "being of one mind" and friendship in Hellenistic literature. Hence on this point Paul's texts are of little help; they neither confirm nor weaken our hypothesis that Luke's notion of Christian unity is related to Greek theories of friendship.

Union of Souls and Community of Goods

Acts 4:32 creates the impression, as we have already noticed, that some connection exists between unity of heart and soul, on the one hand, and the early Christian practice of holding everything in common, on the other. We may hope to discover something more about the nature of this connection from the data of Christian exhortation. A brief sampling of evidence will have to suffice.

A. Let us consider first of all the argument *a fortiori* presented in two closely related texts, one from the *Didache* and the other from the *Epistle of Barnabas*. In the first of these we read:

> You shall not turn away the man in need (*ton endeomenon*), but you shall share all things in common (*sygkoinoneseis de panta*) with your brother, and you will not say that they are your own goods (*ouk ereis idia einai*). For if you share (*koinonoi este*) the imperishable good, how much the more should you share goods that are perishable (*Didache* 4:8).

And the second text runs:

> You shall share all things in common (*koinoneseis en pasin*) with your neighbor, and you shall not say that they are your own (*ouk ereis idia einai*). For if you share (*koinonoi este*) the incorruptible good, how much the more will you share corruptible goods (*Epistle of Barnabas* 19:8).

Christian *koinonia* is essentially based on the fact that we enjoy the same divine goods. These goods, shared by all, are the objective foundation of fraternal communion among all Christians. A communion this deeply grounded involves by its very nature the obligation to share one's temporal goods with those who are in temporal need. This reflection common to the *Didache* and to the *Epistle of Barnabas* goes further than Luke does in explicitating the inner relationship between union of heart and soul and community of goods and in assigning a natural priority to the former.

B. Paul gives the same idea a slightly different application when discussing the question of the sharing of goods that should take place between Hellenistic-Christian churches and the church of Jerusalem. He explains to the Romans that the Gentiles, in sending relief to the poor of Jerusalem, would be merely repaying a debt: since the Gentiles received a share (*ekoinonesan*) in the spiritual goods of the Jews, they are obliged to assist the Jews in turn with their own temporal goods (Romans 15:27). In the Second Letter to the Corinthians, Paul's viewpoint is slightly different: the Corinthians are to aid the saints in Jerusalem by their temporal goods, so that the latter may help them spiritually in return (2 Corinthians 8:14; 9:12-14). In this way, Paul explains, it will be possible to bring about the "equality" (*isotes*) that should exist among Christians. The model for this equality may be found in the story of the manna which the Israelites ate in the wilderness: "He who had gathered much had nothing superfluous, and he who had gathered a small amount did not lack anything" (Exodus 16:18; 2 Corinthians 8:15). Lietzmann's comment is appropriate: "The normative principle of reciprocal aid is the *isotes*, of which the descriptions in Acts 2:44f., 4:26f., 5, present an ideal image."

Despite the example drawn from Exodus, the notion of "equality" is not biblical; it is typically Greek. The contexts in which the term is used endow it with quite different shades of meaning. It may refer to mathematical equality or to legal equality; it may designate the political equality characteristic of the democratic ideal, or the moral equality that makes harmony among friends possible and that grows by the give-and-take of friendship. The precise sense in which Paul uses the term is not clear, yet it is striking to rediscover at this point in his writings one of the essential themes of friendship.

For friendship is defined precisely by the proverb "friendship is equality" (*isotes philotes*), just as well as by the other maxims "one soul" and "among friends all is common." These three proverbs are complementary. Equality begets friendship, as it creates between friends the harmony and union of minds that make of them "one single soul." It supposes an exchange and a sharing that extend naturally to material goods: among friends "everything is shared." Friendship is prior to the moral community of goods; it is their harmony and unity of soul that make friends share everything they have. This sharing, which is a sign and effect of friendship, is also the concrete touchstone of friendship, and the means by which friendship grows. Friendship strives to express itself, and by its self-expression it achieves still more perfect equality and union of souls.

We have been trying to define the relationship between the two parts of Acts 4:32. The perspectives we have just presented help us to grasp that relationship. Union of hearts and souls is a prior condition among Christians which impels them to pool their possessions. Yet sharing their goods also facilitates the full development of genuine union of souls. Thus union of souls is at once the cause and the effect of an attitude by reason of which each individual considers his goods as belonging to all.

CONCLUSIONS

A. The *koinonia* which Acts 2:42 tells us the first Christians assiduously practiced is explained by other passages in Acts which describe them as holding "everything in common" (2:44; 4:32). This *koinonia* does not consist just in the fact that they share (*metechein*) together the same goods, nor simply in the solidarity that results from this common sharing. It acquires an active dimension as well: Christians draw the consequences of their solidarity by persevering in the practice of *koinonia*, by continuing to pool whatever they possess. Their attitude is diametrically opposed to the individualistic selfishness of "each one for himself." They are concerned for others, following the example of Christ, who "rich as he was, made himself poor for us, so as to enrich us by his poverty" (2 Corinthians 8:9; cf. Philippians 2:4; 1 Corinthians 10:24, 33; 13:5; Romans 15:2). This *koinonia* consists, more specifically, in putting whatever one has at the disposal of those in need, without reserving anything for oneself. Thus it is the concrete manifestation and the sensible sign of unity of hearts and souls.

B. There are reasons for thinking that into his description of early Christian fellowship Luke incorporates and transposes Greek and Hellenistic literary themes relating to friendship. Though the evidence for this is not absolutely compelling, yet it seems strong enough to justify the hypothesis we have presented. That hypothesis helps us understand better the precise shape that Luke has given to his descriptions of early Christian community life.

C. We must notice, however, that Luke carefully avoids calling the first Christians "friends," although he does not hesitate to employ this term in other contexts. He does not even generally call them "brothers," but simply "believers." This fact would seem to suggest that our starting point for an explanation of early Christian behavior should be the faith by which they are all joined to Christ and united to one another. This faith is the ground of their fellowship, the foundation of their *koinonia.*

D. Neither does Acts employ the vocabulary of love. Yet in the descriptions of *koinonia* in Acts we immediately recognize the expression and concrete manifestation of that fraternal charity which ought to animate Christians. This is clear not only from Luke's probable use of the theme of friendship in the passages we have been considering, but also from the exhortations we mentioned above, particularly Philippians 1:27 and 2:2. Thus Luke's descriptions of early Christian *koinonia* present an illustration of Christian charity, which involves inseparably both union of souls and fraternal sharing with those who are in need. It would be inaccurate to imagine the Christians of Acts as striving merely for generosity in the practice of almsgiving, or even as striving, under the impulse of eschatological expectation, toward an ideal of ascetical renunciation or detachment from worldly goods. The ideal for which they strove was rather Christian charity itself.

And in that primitive community's experience of love, the ancient Greek ideal of friendship achieved, upon unexpected new foundations, its own concrete realization.

Messianic Interpretation
of the Psalms
in the Acts of the Apostles

Quotations from the Old Testament within the Book of Acts are of interest from several points of view. For instance, these quotations constitute a privileged area for textual criticism. They also promise to shed some light on the composition of Acts as a whole, and especially on the speeches attributed to the main actors in the story. Further, the stereotyped formulas that introduce these citations reveal the thinking of the early Church about the origin, both divine and human, of the inspired Scriptures. In the present study, however, it will be necessary for us to limit ourselves to one of the many possible aspects of this topic. We will turn our attention exclusively to quotations from the Psalter in Acts, and within that area we will be concerned with a single question: *How does the Acts of the Apostles interpret the passages it cites from the Psalms?* We hope, of course, that this study of a selected sampling of material will contribute significantly to our understanding of a larger question: the nature of Old Testament exegesis as practiced in the early Christian Church.

By way of introduction we will offer some preliminary observations about the material to be investigated and about various tendencies in Christian interpretation of the psalms. In our central section, we will analyze in some detail those direct citations and obvious allusions to psalms which are christologically interpreted within Acts. Finally we will conclude our investigation with a few remarks of a more general nature about the method and value of this early Christian exegesis of the psalms.

I. PRELIMINARY OBSERVATIONS

The Data

A. The Acts of the Apostles contains *seven explicit quotations* from the psalms. Of these, two are to be found in Peter's remarks prior to the election of Matthias to take the place of Judas (1:20), two in Peter's speech at Pentecost (2:25-28, 34), two in Paul's inaugural speech at Antioch in Pisidia (13:33, 35), and, finally, one in the prayer of the apostles after their appearance before the Sanhedrin (4:25-26).

B. A list of the *implicit quotations* from the psalms within Acts is more difficult to draw up. It seems necessary to make a clear distinction from the beginning of our inquiry. We may speak of an implicit citation, an allusion, or a reminiscence only in cases where the text of Acts allows us to establish, with a greater or lesser degree of probability, that this or that specific passage from the psalms is really being alluded to or recalled. Whenever we cannot show such an intentional allusion, passages from the psalms that exhibit interesting similarities with expressions in Acts should be considered as simple parallels. Similarity in vocabulary or thought content does not necessarily imply real cross-reference. And since merely parallel passages do not permit us to draw any conclusions about the Christian interpretation of a psalm, it seems wise to limit our study to clearly intentional citations.

This principle allows us to reduce considerably the list of citations from the psalms within Acts that is sometimes drawn up. We will retain for examination only eight implicit citations. Of these, five will be found within the speeches of Peter (2:30, 33a, 33b-34a; 4:11; 5:31), two in Stephen's speech (7:46, 55-56), and one in Paul's discourse at Antioch in Pisidia (13:22).

The reader may already have noticed that all of the quotations mentioned, whether explicit or implicit, occur in the first part of Acts, and also that all of them are attributed to the apostles, Peter, Paul and Stephen.

C. Another significant point, which it will be sufficient to mention briefly here, is the fact that Acts quotes the psalms according to *the Greek translation of the Septuagint.* Despite slightly variant readings, which are easy to explain, there can be no doubt about the provenance of the explicit citations. In the case of the implicit citations the evidence is less striking; yet the assertion that they, too, are derived from the Greek Bible is based on sufficiently significant clues. We may take it as established, therefore, that the exegesis of the psalms within the Acts of the Apostles is based upon the Greek Psalter. Nevertheless, to facilitate the task of the reader, we shall follow the practice generally adopted in modern translations and designate the individual psalms according to the Hebrew numbering system.

Two Types of Interpretation

In the inventory of fifteen citations or allusions to psalms within the Acts of the Apostles which we have drawn up, not all the texts are of equal interest to us. When we review those citations to get an initial global impression of the kind of interpretation they represent, we quickly discover two quite distinct types of interpretation, on the basis of which we are able to divide the texts into two, rather unequal, groups. On the one hand, there is an interpretation which we may call "historical" and which is exemplified in only three of the fifteen passages. On the other, we meet a type of interpretation which may properly be called "messianic" or "christological" and which is represented in the remainder, the overwhelming majority, of the texts. A word about each of these two types will be useful:

A. The *historical* interpretation is found in the following three passages: (1) the allusion to Psalm 132:11 in the Pentecost discourse (2:30), (2) the allusion to Psalm 132:5 in Stephen's speech (7:46), and (3) the allusion to Psalm 89:21 in Paul's discourse at Antioch in Pisidia (13:22).

The context in these cases involves a survey of the events in the history of Israel. Once the survey arrives at the figure of David, allusions to his story are drawn not merely from information supplied by the properly historical books, but also from the Psalter. Thus the psalms, too, are considered source material for the history of David, their presumed author. In this kind of interpretation the psalms are not exploited as oracles pointing to the future but purely as historical documents. They are cited because of the factual data they contain about events of past history—data guaranteed, of course, by the authority of the writings in which they are recorded. This method of reading the psalms, which goes to the Psalter simply to gather information about David as an individual, raises no problems for our study, but falls outside of our field of interest. It is sufficient to have noted its presence in Acts, without lingering over it at any greater length.

B. The other twelve citations from the Psalter in Acts, whether explicit or implicit, all exemplify a *messianic* or *christological* interpretation, one which reads the psalms for information not about David, but about the Messiah. In fact, in exegesis of this type the early Church applies to Christ, specifically to his passion and resurrection, a whole series of statements from the psalms which have nothing to do with David at all. In early Christian thinking the psalms spoke of the Messiah; they contained prophecies which were fulfilled in the passion and resurrection of Jesus. In order to discover the true meaning of the psalms, all the early Christians had to do was compare their content with the details of these still recent events.

The following section will be devoted to detailed examination of the twelve texts which concern us. We hope that our analysis will bring to light the presuppositions of this christological interpretation of the psalms and will demonstrate precisely how this early Christian exegetical method worked.

II. EXEGESIS OF INDIVIDUAL PSALMS

Psalm 16:10

A. Sound method suggests that we should start with the clearest example. This is to be found in Peter's speech at Pentecost, in the interpretation he offers there of the statement from Psalm 16:10: "You will not abandon my soul to Hades, nor suffer your Holy One to see corruption." Luke has gone to the trouble of transcribing the context at some length, citing four verses from the

psalm in their entirety, because the whole passage, and not simply
the statement of verse 10, appears to refer to Christ:

> For David says concerning him [Jesus],
> "I saw the Lord always before me,
> for he is at my right hand that I may not be shaken;
> therefore my heart was glad, and my tongue rejoiced;
> moreover my flesh will dwell in hope.
> For you will not abandon my soul to Hades,
> nor let your Holy One see corruption.
> You have made known to me the ways of life;
> you will make me full of gladness with your presence."
> (Psalm 16:8-11, Acts 2:25-28, RSV)

From this passage it is especially verse 10, "For you will not
abandon my soul to Hades, etc.," which supplies the basis for
Peter's line of reasoning; indeed he cites that same verse from the
psalm a second time in verse 27, and echoes its vocabulary once
again in verse 31. The presence of the word "flesh" in this final
allusion, in place of the expression "Holy One" which we have been
led by this time to expect, shows that Peter has also been influenced
by the statement of the psalm just prior to the crucial verse 10 as
well: "my *flesh* will dwell in hope" (Psalm 16:9).

Peter's argumentation rests upon the underlying supposition
that Psalm 16 is speaking of a resurrection in the strict sense of the
term. This supposition he does not attempt to demonstrate; he
accepts it as quite self-evident and requiring no justification. Clearly
this postulate could be discussed, and we might legitimately question whether Peter has precisely grasped the sense of the original
Hebrew text, or even of the Greek translation. The Hebrew for
"You will not abandon my soul to Sheol (*lesheol*)" has been translated literally into Greek as "You will not abandon my soul to
Hades (*eis haden*)," which may not be the exact equivalent of "You
will not abandon my soul *in* Hades." Peter is obviously not concerned, however, with the meaning of those terms in themselves,
nor with scrupulously determining the original intention of the
psalmist. He thinks of resurrection spontaneously, because the language of the psalm reminds him of the resurrection of Jesus. The
meaning of the psalm for him is not determined by detailed analy-

sis, but by comparison with the Easter event, which casts its own light on the text of the psalm and brings it into fresh relief.

On the supposition, therefore, that the psalm does speak of a resurrection, Peter can develop his line of thought. His intention is to establish that when David, the author of the psalm, expressed confidence that he would rise from the dead, he was in fact speaking of the Christ: *legei eis auton* (v. 25). Peter proceeds in two stages, mentioning first a negative consideration and thereafter a positive one. The negative consideration is found immediately after the extended citation from the psalm:

> Brethren, I may say to you confidently of the patriarch David, that he both died and was buried, and his tomb is with us to this day (v. 29).

The text of Psalm 16:10 cannot apply to David personally, since it was not fulfilled in his individual case; instead, David died and was buried, and his grave can still be seen as evidence of that. Peter's positive consideration is more fully developed and itself involves two phases:

> Being therefore a prophet, and knowing that God had sworn with an oath to him that he would set one of his descendants upon his throne, he foresaw and spoke of the resurrection of the Christ, that he was not abandoned to Hades, nor did his flesh see corruption. This Jesus God raised up, and of that we are all witnesses (vv. 30-32).

Peter begins by showing that it was possible for David to speak of the Christ. Since David had received the promise that the Christ would be born from his own descendants, he knew that the Christ would come; he had learned of him through the oracle of Nathan, which is mentioned in Psalm 132:11, a text which Peter recalls in our present context (v. 30). Nathan, however, had not predicted the resurrection of the Christ. David's knowledge on this point must be attributed to his prophetic charism: since David himself was a prophet, he had the gift of foreseeing the future and thus he was able to know beforehand that the Messiah would rise from the dead (v. 31a). Peter concludes by emphasizing the fact that the oracle of Psalm 16:10 has been fulfilled in Jesus (v. 31b): since Jesus was raised from the dead, he did not remain in Hades, and his flesh did not see corruption. Therefore he is really the Messiah of whom the psalm was speaking.

To help us understand Peter's reasoning clearly, it may be useful to spell out more explicitly the connection between the negative consideration of verse 29 and the double positive consideration of verses 30-31. It is not sufficient merely to assert that the terms of the psalm do not apply to David because he personally did not emerge from his tomb. It is necessary to consider a further detail. David speaks in the first person in the psalm, as if he were indeed referring to himself, and we cannot suppose that, though he employs the pronoun "I," he is in fact referring to someone completely other than himself. The someone else referred to, though it may not be David in person, must nevertheless be somehow identical with him. And this is precisely the case with the Messiah, who is the new David and also his son. It is this close bond between David and his messianic descendant which enables the holy king to speak of the Messiah as if he were speaking of himself. This mode of expression finds its foundation and justification in the prophecy of Nathan, which predicts that the Messiah will come from David's own offspring. And regarding this other self David also knows, by virtue of his own prophetic charism, that he will rise from the dead.

The precise point of Peter's reasoning must be accurately grasped. It is often asserted that Peter desires to prove that Jesus has really risen from the dead, but that is obviously inaccurate, for Peter presupposes the resurrection as a datum of faith. What Peter wishes to establish is rather the fact that Jesus, having really risen from the dead, is truly the Messiah of which the psalm speaks. The real conclusion of the argumentation is to be found in the solemn affirmation: "By raising Jesus from among the dead, God has made him the Christ" (v. 36). Peter's point is the messianic character of Jesus. The resurrection is a sign which points to Jesus' messiahship. And the resurrection owes its value as a sign precisely to the oracle of the psalm which announced that the Christ would rise.

Finally, we need scarcely emphasize the obvious fact that Peter's interpretation of Psalm 16, though scrupulously logical and internally coherent, moves entirely within the perspective of Christian faith; it is interpretation *ex fide in fidem.* It is the Easter experience of the early Christians that enables them to discover the genuine meaning of the Scriptures. Thereafter they can recognize in the psalms an expression of their own faith that Jesus is the Christ and can employ them as a means of communicating that faith to others.

B. We find a second instance of the use of Psalm 16:10 in Paul's discourse at Antioch in Pisidia. Paul, however, quotes only the second part of the verse, "You will not allow your Holy One to see corruption" (13:35); and his argumentation centers on the word "corruption" (*diaphthora*, vv. 34, 35, 36, 37), which may be a questionable translation of the Hebrew noun *shahat*.

Paul's speech opens with a rapid survey of some episodes in the early history of Israel from the Exodus down to the time of David (13:16-22). At that point, in connection with David and in language influenced by 2 Samuel 7:12, Paul alludes to the prophecy of Nathan as a prophecy already fulfilled: "Of this man's posterity God has brought to Israel a Savior, Jesus, as he promised" (v. 23). Then, after briefly outlining the events of the Gospel story (vv. 24-31), Paul returns to the theme of prophecy fulfilled: "And we bring you the good news that what God promised to the fathers, this he has fulfilled to us their children by raising Jesus" (vv. 32-33a).

To support this affirmation Peter appeals to a number of biblical passages in rapid succession (vv. 33b-35):

> . . . as also it is written in the second psalm, "Thou art my Son, today I have begotten thee" (Psalm 2:7). And as for the fact that he raised him from the dead, no more to return to corruption, he spoke in this way, "I will give you the holy and sure blessings of David" (Isaiah 55:3). Therefore he also says in another psalm, "Thou wilt not let thy Holy One see corruption" (Psalm 16:10).

After citing the first of these texts, Psalm 2:7, Paul formulates a new introduction to his scriptural argument in language influenced by the wording of Psalm 16:10 (v. 34a), but the quotation from Psalm 16:10, for which we have thus been prepared, is held in suspense while Paul first cites the very enigmatic text from Isaiah 55:3. Only after this delay, and with the aid of another introductory formula, does Paul finally quote Psalm 16:10 (v. 35).

We will deal with the texts of Psalm 2:7 and Isaiah 55:3 in their proper places. But for the moment we are concerned exclusively with Psalm 16:10, and it is this text in fact which supplies

Paul with the ground and foundation for the messianic reflections that he presents to his audience in the following verses:

> For David, after he had served the counsel of God in his own genera-
> tion, fell asleep, and was laid with his fathers, and saw corruption; but
> he whom the Lord raised up saw no corruption (vv. 36-37).

Paul's first consideration is negative, analogous to that of Peter at 2:29. David died and saw corruption, and hence, Paul implies, the statement of the psalm cannot refer to him personally. However, Paul continues immediately with the positive assertion: "but he whom God raised up saw no corruption" (v. 37). We recall that Peter, after showing that the prophecy does not apply to David, had given reasons for thinking that it applies to David's messianic descendant. Though Paul does not develop this positive consider-ation as explicitly as Peter did, yet it is not entirely absent from his exposition, for he refers several times in the present context to God's promise to David (vv. 23 and 32). And it is precisely this promise which justifies our applying to Christ statements like Psalm 16:10, which appear to refer to David but which do not in fact apply to his own personal experience.

Obviously Paul's reasoning at Antioch in Pisidia involves the same presuppositions as Peter's at Pentecost. The use of Psalm 16:10 in these two speeches illustrates a feature of early Christian exegesis, namely that the first Christians made no effort to deter-mine whether the psalm had originally spoken of a resurrection in the proper sense of that term. Such a question does not even seem to have occurred to them. That meaning simply comes spontane-ously and inevitably to their minds when they read that verse with the events of Easter fresh in their memories. And once they have noticed the marvelous correspondence between David's prediction and Jesus' resurrection, they naturally feel free to employ that verse from the psalm as one more argument to show that Jesus really is the object of the messianic promise.

Psalm 110:1

A. Let us now turn back again to Peter's speech at Pentecost, and to the precise point at which we left it a few moments ago. For immediately after his christological application of Psalm 16:10 to

Jesus' resurrection, Peter goes on to introduce into his discourse a citation from another psalm:

> This Jesus God raised up, and of that we are all witnesses. Being therefore exalted at the right hand of God, and having received from the Father the promise of the Holy Spirit, he has poured out this which you see and hear. For David did not ascend into the heavens; but he himself says, "The Lord said to my Lord, Sit at my right hand, till I make thy enemies a stool for thy feet" (Psalm 110:1). Let all the house of Israel therefore know assuredly that God has made him both Lord and Christ, this Jesus whom you crucified (Acts 2:32-36, RSV).

If the text of Psalm 110:1 is to serve Peter's purpose, it must be pressed into the service of the Christian faith, as Psalm 16:10 was, and made to point to Christ and to speak, at least implicitly, of his resurrection. We will see that Peter's treatment of this psalm is, in fact, quite similar to the treatment we observed in the case of the previous psalm; here, too, Peter's considerations have both a negative and a positive aspect.

Negatively, Peter notices that Psalm 110:1 does not refer to David personally. Since Peter does accept David as the person speaking in this text (*legei de autos*, v. 34), he might have based his argument at this point on the fact that David speaks of someone whom he calls "my Lord," a feature of the text to which Jesus drew attention in his famous discussion about the relation between David and the Messiah (Luke 20:44 and par.). But instead Peter remains true to the Easter perspective which dominates his speech and draws his argument from that: "It was not David who ascended into the heavens" (v. 34). This observation corresponds to the remark of verse 29 above: since David died and was buried and never left his tomb, it is clear that he has not ascended into the heavens, and therefore he cannot be seated at the right hand of God. This means that God's command, "Sit at my right hand," cannot have been addressed to David.

Positively, Peter tries to show that this command, enunciated in Psalm 110:1, was addressed to Jesus. Not only did God raise Jesus from the dead, as is demonstrated by the testimony of the apostles (v. 32), but Jesus also ascended into heaven, as is proved by the fact that he has poured out the Spirit upon his disciples. He could not have given them the Spirit until he had himself received it from the Father; and in order to receive it from the Father, it was necessary that he first ascend to him in heaven. This line of reasoning (vv. 33-34) recalls the language of Psalm 68:19, a text which is applied in Ephesians 4:8 to Christ's ascension: "You ascended on high, you led captivity captive, you received gifts for man" (LXX). Allusion to this supplementary text here increases the probative force of Peter's argument: Jesus, unlike David, did "ascend" on high, and he "received" from God the gift of the Spirit, which he has just poured out. Therefore this outpouring of the Spirit is a sign of his heavenly ascension. Consequently Peter has no difficulty applying to Jesus the words of Psalm 110:1: since he has ascended into heaven, he is now seated at the right hand of God. And finally it is natural to conclude that Jesus is therefore the "Lord" (v. 36), the one whom God invited, according to Psalm 110:1, to take his place at his own right hand.

There are several assumptions implicit behind this interpretation as well. The one whom David designates in the address "my Lord" is and can only be the messianic sovereign, and Peter does not judge it necessary to spell this out in so many words. It also seems self-evident to him that this messianic ruler can take his place at God's right hand only after having ascended into the heavens, for is not God's throne in heaven? Such details as these are not derived from Psalm 110. They all fit so neatly together in Peter's mind with the details that are found in the psalm only because he reads the text of the psalms with recent events still fresh in his memory. Once again it is the Easter experience of the disciples which is opening the meaning of the texts for them. And inversely, it is these texts which enable them to grasp the deep and transcendent meaning of the events they have witnessed. We might say that the texts reveal the heavenly side of those events.

B. This same passage, Psalm 110:1, which was cited and explained by Peter in his speech at Pentecost, was also recalled by Stephen in a statement that unleashed upon him the wrath of his enemies and led to his death. At the end of Stephen's speech, his hearers

> ... were enraged, and they ground their teeth against him. But he, full of the Holy Spirit, gazed into heaven, and he saw the glory of God, and Jesus standing at the right hand of God; and he said,

"Behold, I see the heavens opened, and the Son of Man standing at the right hand of God." But they cried out with a loud voice and stopped their ears and rushed together upon him. Then they cast him out of the city and stoned him (Acts 7:54-58a).

There is a clearly deliberate parallelism between Stephen's description of his vision (v. 55) and Jesus' important declaration before the Sanhedrin in the Synoptic passion narratives. Mark gives Jesus' statement in these terms: "You will see the Son of Man sitting at the right hand of the Power, and coming with the clouds of heaven" (Mark 14:62). Mark's formula, like the quite similar one in Matthew 26:64, combines allusions to two texts: first to the text of Daniel 7:13, where the Son of Man is said to come with the clouds of heaven, and secondly to the text of Psalm 110:1, which speaks of the Lord sitting at the right hand of God. Luke's parallel is slightly shorter: "From now on the Son of Man shall be seated at the right hand of the power of God" (Luke 22:69). We notice that Daniel's image of the Son of Man coming on the clouds of heaven has disappeared from this version; Luke retains the figure of the Son of Man from Daniel, but he is satisfied to describe him simply as sitting at the right hand of God, a feature derived from Psalm 110.

In Stephen's vision (7:55-56) we recognize the figure of the Son of Man from Daniel, and he is occupying a position "at the right hand of God," as in the psalm. Luke does not specify, however, that the Son of Man is "seated" in Stephen's vision; he simply "is at God's right hand," doubtless in a standing position. In this posture Luke seems to capture a picture of the Son of Man at a moment between the action of his sitting at God's side, described in the psalm, and the action of his coming, mentioned in Daniel. Therefore the only trace of Psalm 110:1 which clearly remains in Stephen's vision is the detail that Jesus is "at God's right hand." This detail is typical enough, however, to enable us to count Acts 7:55-56 as one more instance of an allusion to a psalm which was quite familiar to the early Christians.

Hence we may say, in summary, that the early Church, aware of the fact that after his resurrection Jesus ascended into heaven, discovered in Psalm 110 the meaning of that ascension: Jesus has been enthroned in his glory as Lord, as the One to whom God gives the command, "Sit at my right hand!"

Psalm 2:7

We have already noted that both Peter and Paul, in their respective "inaugural addresses" within Acts, utilize Psalm 16 in an effort to demonstrate from Scripture that the risen Jesus is really the Messiah. And we have just seen that Peter reinforces his argument from Psalm 16 at Pentecost by another argument based on Psalm 110. Similarly Paul at Antioch in Pisidia couples two texts from the psalms together, leading into his argument from Psalm 16 by citing beforehand Psalm 2:7.

The precise significance of this citation is not immediately apparent in itself, and Paul does not pause to explain it. Fortunately, however, we are able to find clear clues to the meaning of this text for the early Church from the context in which it is cited, and especially from the statement by which it is introduced (Acts 13:32-33):

> We bring you the good news that what God promised to the fathers, this he has fulfilled to us their children by raising Jesus, as also it is written in the second psalm, "Thou art my Son, today I have begotten thee" (Psalm 2:7).

The divine promise to which Paul alludes (v. 32) can only be the one that is recalled earlier in the present context (vv. 22-23): God has promised to raise a Savior for Israel from the posterity of David, as is known from Nathan's oracle.

We may wonder why Paul should quote Psalm 2 here at all. Why isn't he satisfied simply to refer to Nathan's oracle itself? It would have been easy enough, for instance, to echo the language of the oracle directly, "I will raise up your offspring after you" (2 Samuel 7:12), exploiting again the ambiguity of the Greek verb for "raise up," which, as we have seen, can also mean "raise from the dead."

A passage from the Epistle to the Hebrews may help us answer this question and clarify Paul's point. The opening verses of that letter, dealing with the resurrection and exaltation of Jesus, combine explicit citations from the prophecy of Nathan (2 Samuel 7:14) and Psalm 2:7:

> ... he sat down at the right hand of the Majesty on high, having become as much superior to the angels as the name he has obtained is more excellent than theirs. For to what angel did God ever say, "Thou art my Son, today I have begotten thee" (Psalm 2:7), or again, "I will be to him a father, and he shall be to me a son" (2 Samuel 7:14)? (Hebrews 1:3-5)

By the juxtaposition of these two texts the author focuses attention clearly on the new name, the title "Son," which was conferred on Jesus at his resurrection when he took his seat at the right hand of God and became superior to the angels. There is no suggestion of an adoptionist christology in these verses, although unjustifiable interpretation of their language within the categories of Greek philosophy has sometimes led to misunderstanding on this point. The christology expressed here is grounded not in Greek philosophy but in an understanding of the Easter event, and the viewpoint is quite similar to that of Peter at Pentecost: by raising Jesus up, God made him "Lord" and "Christ" (Acts 2:23), and by the same action he constituted him "Son of God" (Hebrews 1:4-5). These various titles express the transcendent royal dignity conferred on Jesus in his humanity, when God seated him on his throne and gave him all power in heaven and on earth. The author of Hebrews discovers this mystery of the Easter glorification of Jesus both in Nathan's oracle, in which God promised that he would make David's descendant his own son (2 Samuel 7:14), and in Psalm 2, where the prophecy is even clearer: on the day on which he is consecrated King in Zion, the Anointed of the Lord becomes the Son of God and receives the assurance of universal dominion (Psalm 2:2, 6-7, 8ff.).

These royal overtones in the language of Psalm 2 also explain its use in Acts 13:33, the text we have been considering. Here, too, the context involves a treatment of the theme of Jesus' glorification at the moment of his resurrection. Paul asserts that at Jesus' glorification God fulfilled not only the promise contained in Nathan's oracle, but also the more explicit promise of Psalm 2:7. At his enthronement as Davidic sovereign, Jesus was invested with a power and a glory surpassing all the kings of the earth, which makes him the "Lord" mentioned by Psalm 110 and the "Son of God" announced by Psalm 2. The royal investiture to which each of these texts alludes both presupposes the resurrection and is an immediate consequence of the resurrection. And it is this connection between Jesus' resurrection and his heavenly glorification which enables the early Church to claim that God, by raising Jesus, fulfilled the promise that he would make one of David's descendants his own Son and share with him his own universal kingship.

Since Paul's line of reasoning is expressed in an extremely condensed and elliptical way, it would be difficult to grasp the precise point of Acts 13:33 without the aid of parallels such as Acts 2:36 and Hebrews 1:5. Even the applicability of Psalm 2:7 to the resurrection of Jesus is not obvious unless one accepts the Easter event as a mystery which involves, on its deepest level of significance, a super-earthly, heavenly, dimension. For a Jewish audience which did not already believe in the transcendent lordship of the risen Christ, Paul's argumentation at Antioch would not be at all convincing. For his exegesis of Psalm 2:7 presupposes faith and moves entirely within the sphere of faith. Paul's line of reasoning proceeds, as Peter's does, *ex fide in fidem*, offering an exposition of Christian belief rather than an extrinsic demonstration for it.

Psalm 2:1-2

Early in the story of Acts, Peter and John are arrested for "proclaiming in Jesus the resurrection from the dead." After a night in prison, they are interrogated by the Sanhedrin, but they are eventually released with the warning to preach and teach in the name of Jesus no longer. When the other apostles are informed of this warning and the accompanying threats of the Sanhedrin against the group, they all turn spontaneously to God, asking him for strength and courage. Luke gives us their prayer, which begins (Acts 4:24b-26):

Sovereign Lord, who didst make the heaven and the earth and the sea and everything in them, who by the mouth of our father David, thy

servant, didst say by the Holy Spirit, "Why did the Gentiles rage, and
the peoples imagine vain things? The kings of the earth set themselves
in array, and the rulers were gathered together, against the Lord and
against his Anointed" (Psalm 2:1-2)—

No sooner have the apostles invoked God as the Creator and Lord
of the universe when their prayer immediately incorporates a
citation from the opening verses of Psalm 2, which describe a
conspiracy against the Anointed of the Lord. As the prayer continues, the main terms of this citation are taken up again and worked
into a paraphrase which explains the meaning of the text in more
precise detail:

for truly in this city there were *gathered together* against thy holy
servant Jesus, whom thou didst *anoint*, both Herod and Pontius Pilate, with *the Gentiles* and *the peoples* of Israel, to do whatever thy
hand and thy plan had predestined to take place (vv. 27-28).

Thus "the kings of the earth," of whom the psalm spoke, are
represented by Herod, and "the rulers" by Pontius Pilate. "The
Gentiles" refer to the pagans who played a role in the drama of the
passion, and "the peoples" allude to Israel (provided we are using
the Greek translation, for the reference in the Hebrew original is to
foreign peoples). These enemies of God have all "gathered together" against the Christ.

This detailed exegesis rests upon the basic supposition that the
psalm is speaking of the Christ, that is, of Jesus himself. On this
supposition it is quite easy to identify the individual adversaries of
the Messiah with the principal actors in the passion. The strictly
messianic interest governing this interpretation becomes all the
more apparent when we consider the circumstances in which the
apostles are said to appeal to this passage. Though as they utter
their prayer they are themselves the objects of a persecution insti-
gated by the Sanhedrin (4:1), nevertheless their interpretative commentary on Psalm 2:1-2 does not speak about this persecution or
about their own enemies, the Sadducees, but only of the conspiracy
that led to the death of Jesus. Nor is mention made of any conflicts
between the Christians and Herod (Antipas) or Pontius Pilate. It is
the fate and experience of Christ that they find directly reflected in

the psalms, not that of his disciples, even though they themselves may be undergoing a similar persecution.

The method of interpretation employed in this prayer of the apostles is reminiscent of exegetical procedures that have become familiar to us from the texts of Qumran. It will be useful to cite, by way of example, an excerpt from the Damascus document, which also quotes and comments upon a passage from the Old Testament. In this case the text is that of Deuteronomy 32:33, and it is appealed to in the midst of an invective against the unfaithful Israelites:

> They walk in the way of the godless, of whom God has said, "Their wine is the venom of serpents and the cruel *ro'sh* ('poison' or 'head') of the asps" (Deuteronomy 32:33). The *serpents* are the kings of the peoples, and their *wine* is their ways; and the *head* of the asps is the leader (*ro'sh*) of the kings of Javan, who has come to wreak vengeance on them (CD 8:9-12; 19:22-24).

This exegesis of Qumran involves a play on two possible meanings of the Hebrew word *ro'sh*: the appropriate meaning in the context of Deuteronomy is clearly "poison," but Qumran and later rabbis take the word in its other sense, "head" or "leader." Aside from that, Qumran's interpretation of this passage from Deuteronomy essentially involves simply the application of the ancient text to later circumstances.

A fragment of a "florilegium" discovered in Cave 4 at Qumran, and unfortunately badly damaged, contains a citation from Psalm 2:1-2, along with a commentary upon it, according to which the kings of the nations will stand up, at the end of time, against "the elect of Israel." It would appear as if the expression of the psalm, "against his Anointed One," which is clearly a reference to a single individual, has been interpreted in this text from Qumran in a collective sense. The members of the sect, "the elect of Israel," recognize themselves in the reference to the "Anointed One of the Lord." However that may be, it is certain that Qumran exegesis, though it does not exclude strictly messianic interpretations completely, does enjoy applying to the Qumran community itself Old Testament texts in which Christians would be more likely to find an allusion to the Messiah. For example, Isaiah 28:16 announces that

God will place in Zion a stone that will serve as a foundation. Christians identify this stone with Christ, thereby following the example of the Targum which substitutes the word "king" for the word "stone." Qumran, on the other hand, changes the word "stone" to the plural (1QH VI, 26), or else replaces it with "wall" (1QH VIII, 7-8), so as to facilitate the application of the text to the community.

This comparison with Qumran is instructive, for it helps us to see the radically christological character of early Christian exegesis. In their prayer in Acts 4:27 the apostles give their own interpretation of a sacred text, using methods quite similar to those practiced at Qumran. But in the conspiracy of God's enemies against his Anointed One they spontaneously detect a reference not to the persecution currently afflicting themselves and the Christian community, but to the persecution which led to the death of Jesus. And if the early Christians did, on occasion, apply certain details of texts to other persons, it was always because of the role those persons played in the story of the Messiah. For they were convinced that the psalms spoke of Christ, and they read them to learn about him.

Psalm 69:26 and Psalm 109:8

The first words attributed directly to Peter in Acts are his remarks about Judas' fall from his position as an apostle and the need of finding a replacement for him. In the course of these remarks Peter cites passages from two distinct psalms in which he considers that the fate of Judas had already been predicted by the Holy Spirit, speaking through the mouth of David. This type of interpretation should no longer seem to us merely an arbitrary and superficial accommodation. It should be clear from texts we have already considered that Peter's method is grounded in a theory of interpretation. Precisely because of the role which Jesus' betrayer plays in the passion story, the psalms would be likely to contain prophecies that apply to him. Thus there is no essential difference between this case and that of Psalm 2:1-2, in which early Christians recognized a description of Herod and Pontius Pilate. All of these persons are the objects of prophecies, for the simple reason that the prophecies have to do with Jesus' passion and consequently supply, in passing, details of the parts played by various actors in that drama. In speaking of Christ, therefore, the psalms also have occasion to speak of Judas, just as they do of Herod and Pilate.

Here is the opening portion of Peter's remarks (Acts 1:16-20):

> Brethren, the Scripture had to be fulfilled, which the Holy Spirit spoke beforehand by the mouth of David, concerning Judas who was guide to those who arrested Jesus. For he was numbered among us, and allotted his share in this ministry. (Now this man bought a field with the reward of his wickedness; and falling headlong he burst open in the middle and all his bowels gushed out. And it became known to all the inhabitants of Jerusalem, so that the field was called in their language Akeldama, that is, Field of Blood.) For it is written in the Book of Psalms, "Let his habitation become desolate, and let there be no one to live in it" (Psalm 69:26), and "His office let another take" (Psalm 109:8).

Peter begins by recalling a few facts: the purchase of a property, the ignominious death of the traitor, the horror that clings to the ground that he bought. All these facts signify the fulfillment of a prophecy, which Peter cites in a modified form that facilitates its application to the case at hand: "Let his habitation become desolate, and let there be no one to live in it" (Psalm 69:26). To grasp this interpretation it is essential to remember that Psalm 69 is one of the great passion psalms, in which Christians came to recognize the future sufferings of Christ in the trials endured by the psalmist. In the present case the psalmist also alludes to his enemies and hurls curses at them. Moreover, an incidental detail made it easy for the early Christians to identify the leader of those enemies with Judas, for the curse that the psalm invokes upon that enemy's land corresponds to what actually happened to Judas' property. This application of the text, though perhaps surprising to us, remains nevertheless within the perspective of interpretation based on the supposition that the psalm in its entirety is a prophecy of Jesus' passion.

After citing Psalm 69:26 as a prediction fulfilled in Judas' story, Peter immediately quotes another oracle which has not yet been fulfilled: "His office let another take" (Psalm 109:8). Though Psalm 109 is not one of those habitually quoted in connection with

Jesus' passion, it is a psalm that describes the sufferings of an innocent righteous man. Since Christians recognized prophecies of Christ's sufferings in the similar descriptions of innocent suffering in Psalm 69 and Psalm 22, it is not at all surprising that they should have interpreted Psalm 109 in the same way. This would have made it quite natural for them to apply the curse against a treacherous friend from Psalm 109:8 to Judas. The application of this particular verse to the fallen apostle illustrates again the general principle that the psalms speak of the Christ and his sufferings in the passion.

Psalm 118:22

We have already had occasion to refer to the interrogation of Peter and John by the Sanhedrin after the cure of the lame man at the gate of the temple. The interrogation opens with the question of the priestly leaders to them, "By what power or by what name did you do this?" To this, Peter, under the inspiration of the Holy Spirit, responds:

> Rulers of the people and elders, if we are being examined today concerning a good deed done to a cripple, by what means this man has been healed, be it known to you all and to all the people of Israel, that by the name of Jesus Christ of Nazareth, whom you crucified, whom God raised from the dead, by him this man is standing before you well. This is the stone which was scorned by you builders, but which has become the head of the corner (Psalm 118:22). And there is salvation in no one else, for there is no other name under heaven given among men by which we must be saved (Acts 4:8b-12).

Peter explains that the healing is attributable to the name of Jesus, that is, to the supernatural power with which his name is endowed, and that consequently the miraculous cure testifies to the fact that Jesus, after being crucified, was really raised from the dead (vv. 8-10). Peter then reinforces this statement by an implicit citation from Psalm 118:22 (v. 11).

The citation from Psalm 118:22 does not correspond exactly to the text of the Septuagint. The substitution of the verb "to scorn" (*exoutheneo*) for the verb "to reject" (*apodokimazo*) of the LXX may perhaps be explained by some influence from the language of Isaiah 53:3 ("he was scorned and rejected") upon the present text. In any case it is clear that, within the framework of Peter's speech, the quotation from the psalm repeats in pictorial language what has just been stated in proper terms: "you crucified him/God raised him from the dead; he is the stone you scorned/he has become (i.e., God has made him) the cornerstone." Yet the statement drawn from the psalm also goes beyond the content of the direct, non-metaphorical, statement that preceded it, for in addition to asserting Jesus' resurrection it further declares that his resurrection has made him the "cornerstone." This image is intended to express the dignity bestowed on Jesus at his resurrection; similarly the Aramaic Targum translated "cornerstone" non-metaphorically by the titles of dignity: "king and sovereign." This corresponds concretely to other affirmations in Acts, such as the statement that by raising Jesus, God made him Lord and Christ (2:36), or that Jesus was constituted Son of God by his resurrection (13:33). Therefore Psalm 118:22 was fulfilled on Easter day, in Jesus' heavenly exaltation. By virtue of his royal enthronement at the right hand of God, Jesus became the predicted "cornerstone."

This is confirmed by the concluding remark in Peter's speech (v. 12) that Jesus possesses the only "name" that can assure salvation. This is clearly an allusion to the "name of the Lord," of which Joel says: "Whoever calls upon the name of the Lord will be saved" (Joel 3:5; cf. Acts 2:21). Since Jesus has become the "cornerstone," he is also the "Lord" whose name assures salvation to those who call upon him.

The purpose of the citation in verse 11, therefore, is not to establish the reality of the resurrection, for the miracle that has occurred is for Peter proof enough of that, but to express its significance. Jesus, raised by God, has become the "cornerstone" mentioned in the psalm, and he possesses the name "Lord" of which Joel spoke. What the psalm foretold is now fulfilled: after his rejection by men, Jesus has received from God a dignity without equal. Of course one has to acknowledge this dignity beforehand in order to accept the fact that the oracle has been fulfilled. Since the Jews do not believe in the transcendent lordship of the risen Jesus, Peter's argument will probably leave them quite unmoved. Peter is asserting his faith, rather than demonstrating it. Anyone who shares that faith, however, cannot fail to be struck by the light which the glorified Christ sheds on the text of Psalm 118:22. It is faith in Jesus' lordship that gives Christian preaching its power and persuasiveness.

Psalm 118:16

In two further passages within Acts we may detect the influence of still another verse from Psalm 118, though its influence in these cases is neither so clear nor so certain. Both in his speech at Pentecost and in his defiant confrontation with the Sanhedrin, Peter asserts his faith in the resurrection and then goes on to speak of Jesus' exaltation. The statement about the exaltation in each case contains an identical expression (Greek: *tei dexiai*), which is, however, ambiguous in itself and difficult to translate, so that commentators are divided in their opinions. Here are Peter's two statements:

> Being therefore exalted at/by the right hand of God . . . he has poured out that which you see and hear (Acts 2:33).

> God exalted him at/by his right hand as Leader and Savior (Acts 5:31).

The text of the RSV, which reads "at" in both places, has here been altered to indicate the ambiguity of the original. Are we to understand that God, in raising Jesus up, exalted him *to* his right hand or *by* his right hand? The first of these translations would suggest a deliberate allusion to an Old Testament passage of which we have already spoken above—Psalm 110:1, "The Lord said to my Lord, 'Sit at my right hand.' " The second translation rather recalls a different Old Testament expression, the formula of Psalm 118:16, "The right hand of the Lord has exalted me." Thus it is important to decide between these two possible translations. Is the Greek expression to be construed in a local sense or in an instrumental sense? Let us briefly consider the evidence.

The immediate context, Peter's remarks before the Jewish crowds and before the Sanhedrin, furnishes no decisive clue in favor of either interpretation. Nor does early Christian usage in general offer any help, for both Psalm 110 and Psalm 118 were familiar to the early Christians, and appeal could quite naturally be made to either of them in christological argumentation.

There are, however, several considerations that speak in favor of the instrumental interpretation. First of all, although from a grammatical point of view the expression *tei dexiai* may be understood as a dative of place, yet the dative of place is normally construed with a preposition in New Testament Greek, and in the absence of a preposition the instrumental meaning is preferable: "by the right hand." Secondly, the presence of the verb "to exalt" (*hypsoo*) in both of these citations argues in favor of an allusion to Psalm 118:16, "The right hand of the Lord has exalted me," where the hand of the Lord is the instrument of Jesus' exaltation. Finally, several parallel constructions in Acts invite us to give preference to the instrumental interpretation in the passages that concern us as well. Let us look at these parallels.

1. According to Acts 13:17, "God exalted (*hypsosen*) the people during their stay in the land of Egypt, and with uplifted (*hypselou*) arm he led them out of it." The "exaltation" of the people here corresponds to the "uplifted" arm by which God intervened in their behalf. Similarly Isaiah 63:12 says, also in connection with the Exodus, that God "led Moses by his right hand (*tei dexiai*), the arm of his glory."

2. The statement about the mission God gave Jesus at the moment of his exaltation, namely that "God exalted Jesus by his right hand as Leader and Savior" (Acts 5:31), is comparable to the statement made elsewhere about Moses, namely that "God sent him as both ruler and deliverer by the hand (*syn cheiri*) of the angel that appeared to him in the bush" (Acts 7:35). Moses' mission was entrusted to him, or was to be carried out, "by the hand of the angel that appeared to him and in this case the hand of the angel is clearly an instrument, not a place. The role as "Leader and Savior" allotted to Jesus at the moment of his exaltation is connected with the "right hand of God" (5:31), and in this case too it is more natural to interpret the expression instrumentally rather than locally. Thus the translation "by the right hand of God is preferable" in Acts 5:31. It is also to be preferred at Acts 2:33, since it is

unlikely that the identical expression in two similar contexts would shift its meaning between its first occurrence and the second.

Admittedly, these allusions are fleeting. Peter suggests the language of Psalm 118:16 only in passing, without trying to emphasize the psalm's prophetic character or to show that it was fulfilled at Jesus' resurrection. Yet the allusions are sufficient evidence of a christological interpretation such as is clearly attested by other verses of Psalm 118, interpretation aimed at establishing that Jesus, since he fulfills the prophecies, is really the Messiah whom the prophecies predicted. The prophecy-fulfilling event is not mere emergence from a tomb; it is Jesus' exaltation in heaven that makes him "Leader and Savior," whose position as Lord must be acknowledged. Realization that prophecy has been fulfilled is conditioned upon our first grasping the sign-value of Jesus' resurrection. His resurrection signals his elevation to transcendent dignity. The messianic prophecies reveal the supernatural significance of the Easter mystery, and insight into that mystery enables us to comprehend what it means in concrete details for Jesus, who fulfills the prophecies, really to be the promised Messiah.

III. CONCLUDING REFLECTIONS

Now that we have examined in some detail the way in which the Book of Acts interprets the passages it cites from the psalms, let us conclude with two considerations of a more general nature. First, we shall attempt a final summary description of the method of Christian interpretation with which we have been dealing. Secondly, we will consider whether this method of Scriptural exegesis retains any value for us today.

Christological Exegesis of the Psalms

I have repeatedly emphasized the fact that the point of reference in the use made of psalms in Acts is Christ. I should warn the reader at this point, however, about a possible unjust generalization. We should not go away from this study with the impression that there is only one single form of Christian exegesis of the psalms.

Even within Acts, we have discovered, alongside the twelve passages that interpret the psalms messianically, three other passages that look to the psalms merely for factual information about the story of David. To reach a position from which we would be able to speak of Christian exegesis as such, it would be necessary to broaden our inquiry. The other writings of the New Testament would provide us with further examples of christological exegesis, to be sure, but we would also encounter other types of interpretation, such as the use of the psalms in the service of parenesis or Christian exhortation. We would also have to compare the exegetic procedures of Acts with those of the Jewish *midrashim* or of the commentaries from Qumran. The methods employed are often similar; a specific example which we have already noticed is the device of "actualization," by which older texts are applied to present contemporary circumstances. Yet there are also differences; I believe that comparison with Jewish exegesis would show that the really distinctive feature of Christian interpretation is its essentially christological concern.

Therefore, without intending to reduce Christian exegesis of the psalms exclusively to the messianic type, it seems permissible to say that this is its truly characteristic form, the one which most typically expresses the mentality of the early Christians as they read the psalms. As they read, they look for Christ and search out prophecies pointing to Jesus' passion and resurrection. For they are convinced that the events of Easter are the fulfillment of the oracles that the psalms contain and, consequently, that it is only in the light of Easter that the psalms disclose their true meaning and authentic significance.

If the Easter events enable us to understand the real meaning of the psalms, the inverse is equally true: the psalms make possible a deeper understanding of the paschal mystery. In the psalms God reveals his secret purposes, and those purposes are realized in the sufferings of Christ and his heavenly exaltation. In the psalms Christ expresses, through the mouth of David, his own feelings and attitudes in carrying out the work of our redemption. This is a point worth reflecting on at some length because it has implications for our use of the psalms in our own prayer.

The Psalms in Christian Prayer

When a Jew prays the psalms, he enters into the feelings of David or some other pious psalmist, or he joins in spirit the Levites who sang these songs in the context of the temple liturgy. The viewpoint of Christians who pray the psalms is different. They know that Jesus made the prayer of the psalms his own, and that changes everything. Henceforth we are no longer concerned with David or other psalmists in themselves, for they merely lent their voices to Christ and spoke in his name. Jesus took over their prayers as his own; their supplications became his during the agony of the passion; their songs of thanksgiving became his in the triumph of the resurrection and glorification. The psalms have a new sound. Since Jesus appropriated the psalmists' words, the voice Christians now hear in the psalms, louder and clearer than any other, is the voice of Christ himself.

In the final analysis, then, the psalms are no mere archive of information about the Christ, nor an arsenal of proof-texts that Jesus really is the Messiah. Far more significantly, since they taught Jesus the language he spoke when he prayed, they became his own prayer. Beyond helping us to know our Lord better, therefore, the psalms enable us to enter deeply into Jesus' own mind and heart, and to unite ourselves with him in the prayer he speaks to his Father.

Apologetic Use of the
Old Testament
in the Speeches of Acts

The earliest Christians read their Bible with extremely close attention, and from the beginning Christian preachers urged their audiences to ponder deeply over the texts of the Old Testament, for they were convinced that they could discover in the Scriptures striking testimony to the person, the work and the message of Christ. Those ancient texts cast light on events still fresh in their memories, disclosing to them the full meaning of those events; and, conversely, those ancient prophecies acquired, by reason of their recent fulfillment in Jesus, new contemporary relevance. The meaning of the Old Testament and of Jesus' life and message were discovered simultaneously, and by means of one another. In the course of time, attention came to be focused above all on certain especially striking passages of the Old Testament, out of which there gradually developed a system of Christian apologetics. It is still possible for us today to detect evidence of this process and this early apologetic, for they have left many traces within the speeches in the Acts of the Apostles.

The use of biblical texts for apologetic purposes was not, of course, an innovation of the apostles. Jesus had practiced it before them. We miss the very point of Jesus' teachings if we do not realize that they constantly referred back to Old Testament Scripture. Indeed, Jesus presented himself precisely as the one in whom what Israel had so long been waiting for was finally realized, as the one toward whom all the Scriptures converged. The apostles continued this teaching of Jesus in their own preaching, exploiting the new insights into it which recent events, Jesus' passion and resurrection, gave them.

Significantly it is not in the Book of Acts but in the final chapter of his Gospel that Luke gives us his clearest definition of the systematic use of proof from Scripture among the early Christians. By placing this type of argumentation programmatically on the lips of Jesus at the end of his Gospel, Luke emphasizes as clearly as he can the continuity between the preaching of the apostles and Jesus' own teaching. The Church received directly from her Lord on Easter day the message which she was then to proclaim to the world. Jesus himself gave the two disciples on the road to Emmaus a lesson in Christian hermeneutics (Luke 24:13-32):

> Beginning with Moses and with all the prophets, he interpreted to them in all the Scriptures the things which concerned himself (v. 27).

That same evening he appeared to the apostles, and he opened their minds so that they might understand the Scriptures (v. 45):

> Everything written about me in the Law of Moses and the prophets and the psalms had to be fulfilled (v. 44).

This last statement reads like a comprehensive survey of the divisions of the Hebrew Bible: Jesus mentions first the Pentateuch and then the prophets, first the historical books and then the prophetic writings. Verse 44 further indicates the specific relation between the psalms and collected works of the prophets: since the psalms were considered, in a global way, as the work of David, who was himself a prophet as well as a king, they too are classified as prophetic documents. Thus the demonstration seems to follow the order of the Hebrew Bible itself.

What is the precise point to be demonstrated? Our texts also indicate the answer to that question. To the disciples at Emmaus, for instance, Jesus demonstrated by means of Scripture the necessity "that the Christ should suffer these things and enter into his glory" (v. 26). The same program is described in fuller and more precise detail in Jesus' statement to his apostles that evening:

> Thus it is written that the Christ should suffer and on the third day rise from the dead, and that repentance and forgiveness of sins should be preached in his name to all nations, beginning from Jerusalem (vv. 46-47).

Accordingly, three points from Scripture stand out in high relief: that the Messiah must suffer, that he must rise from the dead, and that the message of salvation must be carried to the whole world, including the pagan nations. The Acts of the Apostles shows that these correspond to the essential points to be demonstrated in the preaching of the apostles. Though we may, on occasion, find texts from the Old Testament applied in other ways and to other points, such applications are secondary. The primary and proper object of early Christian argumentation is quite clearly the three main points mentioned by Jesus to his apostles in the closing scenes of Luke's Gospel.

But how are we to form a concrete idea of this method of argumentation and of the way it works? For that purpose it will be necessary to know exactly which Old Testament texts were employed. In this respect Luke's closing chapter gives us little help, for though he does tell us what purpose the texts are meant to serve, and informs us further that we can find the pertinent texts by reading through the books of the Hebrew Bible in order, he gives us no clue at all here to the precise passages from the Old Testament that the early Christians found most helpful and did in fact employ. Fortunately, however, Luke provides us with a considerable amount of information on these questions in the Acts of the Apostles. Let us turn now to Acts.

We shall not dwell at any length on the many passages within Acts that speak of the general fact that the Christian method of preaching was based on the Scriptures—for example, general allusions to the fact that Paul and other preachers grounded their teaching about Jesus' resurrection on Scripture. Luke quite frequently tells us that the teaching of the apostles was based on Scripture in general, or specifically on the prophets, or on the Law and the prophets combined, or on Moses and the prophets. A number of passages explicitly mention argumentation drawn from Scripture. God is more than once said to have reached such-and-such a decision beforehand and then manifested his designs in Scripture. Finally, two extensive speeches, that of Stephen (ch. 7) and that of Paul at Antioch in Pisidia (ch. 13), are based, at least in part, on a rather systematic examination of the sacred text.

In the pages which follow we shall be concerned exclusively

with the *explicit citations and allusions to Old Testament passages* within the speeches in Acts. And, following the order suggested by Luke 24:44, we shall survey the use made of specific texts from the Law of Moses, from the prophetic writings, and from the psalms. Finally, we shall conclude our study with a number of observations and suggestions of a more general nature.

I. THE LAW OF MOSES

One passage in the books of Moses has attracted special attention because of its christological value. That passage is Deuteronomy 18:15, 18-19, in which God tells Moses that after his death Israel will not be left without an inspired man to announce to it the word of God: "I will raise up for them, from among their kinsmen, a prophet like yourself" (v. 18). When a Christian reads this passage, he interprets the "prophet like Moses" not just as a reference to each and every prophet subsequent to Moses, but specifically to the Christ, the only prophet who is greater than Moses. Hence the importance of the title "prophet" attributed to Jesus in Johannine christology. The Acts of the Apostles cites this passage from Deuteronomy on two occasions, simply quoting it in Stephen's speech (7:37), but using the quotation as an integral part of an argument in Peter's speech after the healing at the gate of the temple (3:22).

What does this text "prove"? The answer is not immediately clear. Peter's speech in Solomon's portico is essentially a proclamation of Jesus' resurrection; it opens with the affirmation that "God has glorified his Servant" (3:13), and it closes with the declaration that "God has raised his Servant up" (3:26). In between these two references to the resurrection, Peter touches on two other topics: the sufferings which Jesus endured and which had been predicted by the prophets (v. 18), and the messianic times which the prophets had also predicted and which Jesus' resurrection suggests may be imminent (v. 21). Now the text of Deuteronomy 18:15ff. does not refer to the sufferings of the Messiah, nor is it directly concerned with the inauguration of the messianic kingdom. We believe that Peter must mean it to refer to the resurrection, because of the ambiguity of the Greek verb *anistemi*, "to lift or raise up," which can mean either "to raise to a position of prominence" or "to raise up from the dead." Peter cites Moses' assurance to the Israelites, "God will *raise up* a prophet for you," and then eventually concludes his speech with the remark, "It is first of all for you that God *raised up* his Servant." Thus the conclusion of Peter's speech directly echoes the citation from Deuteronomy and plays upon the same Greek verb.

Peter's argumentation here distorts the original meaning of Deuteronomy in two ways. First of all the promise to Moses originally meant that God would cause a prophet to be born or to appear, so that Israel would never be without someone to interpret God's will for them, but this promise has now been turned into a messianic prophecy. And secondly, by exploiting the ambiguity of the verb "to raise up," Peter can now make the text a specific prediction of the "resurrection" of the Messiah, a promise that God would raise him from the dead, would bring him back to life.

Deuteronomy goes on to urge the people to "listen to this prophet." That positive exhortation is replaced in Peter's speech by a threat against anyone who refuses to listen to the prophet whom God has raised from the dead. This threat is also drawn from Scripture, but from another context, Leviticus 23:29, where it was originally aimed at those who failed to celebrate the feast of the Atonement. Obviously Peter is employing his Old Testament texts with utmost liberty.

Stephen's speech not only alludes to the same citation from Deuteronomy (Acts 7:37), but it also dwells at length upon the story of Moses, which clearly has figurative significance for him (vv. 17-42). Stephen strongly emphasizes the contrast between the exalted mission that God gave Moses on the one hand, and Israel's constant attitude of rejection and ingratitude toward him on the other. The pivotal text in the treatment of this theme is Exodus 2:14, to which Stephen alludes in verses 27 and 35. Though certain Israelites rejected Moses with the taunt "Who appointed you ruler and judge over us?" yet it was indeed to this same Moses that God had entrusted a mission as "Ruler and Redeemer" (v. 35), with the intention of saving his people through him (v. 25). There is no doubt about the point of Stephen's remarks. Though he is speaking of Moses, he is clearly thinking about Jesus: the attitude of the Jews toward Moses already prefigured their attitude toward the one who was destined to be their Ruler at a later time, the Savior and Redeemer greater than Moses.

This passage from Stephen's speech puts us in a better position to grasp several allusions within the speeches of Peter. Speaking before the Sanhedrin, Peter follows up a reproach addressed to the Jews for their crime against Jesus with the assertion that God, for his part, raised Jesus to the rank of "Ruler and Savior" (5:31). Furthermore, in his earlier remarks in Solomon's portico Peter draws a similar contrast between the actions of the Jews toward Jesus and God's action in his behalf: they "denied" Jesus, even though he was "the prince (literally: the chief) of life," just as they had "denied" Moses (7:35), but God intervened to bring him back to life (3:13-15).

Thus a parallelism is established between Moses and the Christ, which allows the early Christian to apply to the latter what the texts had said of the former, and which prompts them to accentuate certain details of Moses' story that foreshadowed the opposition the Messiah was to encounter from his people. Moses' rejection prefigures the rejection of the Messiah as well.

In this way the events of the exodus become signs of what would occur at the coming of the Messiah (compare 1 Corinthians 10:1-11). As we listen to the exodus story being narrated by Stephen or Paul, we may presume that the details each mentions are not chosen haphazardly, that each is singling out details which have acquired a fresh significance in the light of the Christ event. For instance, Stephen emphasizes the idolatry into which the Israelites fell in the desert (Exodus 32; Acts 7:40-41) in order to prepare his listeners for the idea that their temple is only an image of the true sanctuary, and that God can no more dwell in a sanctuary of human construction (v. 48) than he can be represented by an image of human making (cf. v. 41). By Stephen's selection and presentation of details from the exodus story, the superstitious attachment of the Jews to their temple is made to appear as a continuation of their idolatry in the desert.

There is another apparent allusion to the Pentateuch, this time to a legal text, in the statement that the Jews "hanged Jesus on a tree" (Acts 5:30; 10:39; cf. also 13:29). The recurrence of this expression several times cannot be due to mere chance. We encounter it also in 1 Peter 2:24, and once again in Galatians 3:13, a text which removes any possible doubt about the origin of the expression. It comes from Deuteronomy 21:23. Jesus, hanged upon the tree, was reduced to the situation of one whom the Law called accursed, and thus assumed the curse that the Law uttered against sinners.

We have not yet had anything to say about the Book of Genesis. It is rather difficult to discover any apologetic intention in the story of Abraham as Stephen narrates it to us (7:2-8). On the other hand, the apologetic intention is quite clear in the speech in Solomon's portico in which Peter reports God's promise to Abraham, "In your posterity all the nations of the earth shall be blessed" (Acts 3:25). This promise is recorded in a number of passages, such as Genesis 12:3; 22:18 (compare also 18:18), and is cited in the New Testament at Galatians 3:8 as well. Peter's point is that the messianic blessing, though destined first for the Jews (3:26), must extend to all nations: the risen Christ is a principle of salvation for the Gentiles, too. This is the third point in the program of Christian demonstration from the Scriptures, as set down in Luke 24:46-47.

Stephen's sketch of the story of Joseph the patriarch exhibits a typology similar to that in his Moses narrative, though the point is less strongly pressed. Stephen first recounts how Joseph's brothers, moved by jealousy, sold him to be led away into Egypt (= Genesis 37:11, 28); the vocabulary employed here recalls the crime of the Jews who handed Jesus over to be put to death (3:13; cf. 13:28). Stephen then describes God's action toward Jesus, in pointed contrast to the action of the Jews: "God was with him" (= Genesis 39:2-3, 21-23), as is also said of Jesus in Acts 10:39. God rescued Joseph from all his tribulations and made him ruler of all Egypt and of Pharaoh's own house, and finally Joseph became the savior of his people. Though the correspondence with Christ is not expressed in so many words, we cannot fail to recognize here the pattern that we find so often elsewhere in passages where Jesus is said to have been killed by the Jews but raised up by God and constituted Savior. The behavior of the patriarchs toward Joseph foreshadows the behavior of the Jews toward the Messiah. God's use of events in order to bring glory upon Joseph and make him

Savior of his people points forward to his future intervention on behalf of the Messiah.

At the conclusion of our survey of Pentateuchal allusions within the speeches in Acts, we may state that those speeches quite clearly utilized the stories of both Joseph and Moses. Each of these men was rejected by the Jews and yet entrusted by God with a mission of salvation on behalf of his people. Thus each of them prefigured the fate of the Messiah. These Old Testament figures, and the pattern apparent in their stories, helped early Christian preachers to grasp and reveal the full meaning of Jesus' passion and resurrection.

But the apostolic preaching drew on other texts besides the Joseph and Moses traditions. We have seen that in the promise made to Abraham that all nations would be blessed in his posterity, the early Christians found justification for their mission to the Gentiles. In God's promise to raise up a prophet similar to Moses they also discovered a prediction that God would raise up a prophet from the dead. And finally, they even found, in Deuteronomy 21:23, an allusion to the crucifixion of the Messiah.

II. THE PROPHETS

The Former Prophets

The former prophets, or the works which we should call the historical books, do not require lengthy consideration. Joshua and Judges contributed nothing to the argument from Scripture, and even Samuel, which influenced Luke's infancy narratives, provided no material suitable for the purposes of the apostolic preaching. It is true that Saul is mentioned in one of Paul's speeches in Acts (13:21-22), but he serves merely as a foil for David. Even David himself interested the early preachers mainly in his role as prophet, i.e., as the inspired author of the psalms. They appear to have remembered the historical David as an individual person primarily as the ancestor of the Messiah, the one who received the promise of the Successor toward whom all the hopes of Israel were turned (Acts 2:30; 13:22-23); yet where explicit references to this promise occur, they seem more directly dependent on the psalms than on the Book of Samuel.

Paul's speech at Antioch in Pisidia mentions a parallelism that is worthy of note: just as God raised David as king for the children of Israel, so from David's descendants he raised Jesus for them as Savior (13:22-23). By raising up the Savior, God fulfilled the promise he had made (v. 23), and the continuation of Paul's remarks shows that he understands this promise to refer to the *resurrection* of Jesus, who is established, by reason of his resurrection, in his messianic kingship (v. 33). We recognize in this passage the same double meaning which we pointed out when discussing the text of Deuteronomy 18:15ff.: the idea of "raising up" a leader leads to the idea of "raising up" someone from the dead, since a single Greek verb expresses both ideas. David, raised up by God to be king of Israel, thus becomes a figure of Christ, raised up by God to be Israel's savior (cf. 5:30-31). David's accession to royal dignity comes to be seen as a type of Christ's resurrection and his exaltation to the right hand of God.

The only detail from the story of Solomon mentioned in the speeches is his building of the temple. Stephen alludes to this (7:47), but he does not present Solomon's work as a figure of the work of Christ, since he desires rather to emphasize the contrast between that temple, built by human hands, and the transcendent God, whom no human construction can contain.

In summary, then, it must be admitted that the former prophets, the historical books, are scarcely exploited at all for apologetic purposes within the speeches in Acts. We shall discover quite a different situation, however, in the prophetic writings in the stricter sense, to which we shall now turn.

The Latter Prophets

Joel. Peter's inaugural discourse at Pentecost begins with a long citation from Joel 3:1-5a. The prophet had announced an abundant outpouring of the Spirit for the final times, and Peter asserts that the marvelous experience of the apostles at Pentecost constitutes the realization of that promise (Acts 2:17-21, 33). Joel had declared further that, in order to be saved on that day, one would have to call upon the name of the Lord, and Peter, appealing also to the text of Psalm 110:1, explains that the Lord, whose name is to be invoked, is Jesus whom God raised up (vv. 34-35). It is impossible to exaggerate the importance in primitive christology of the statement from Joel 3:5a, "Whoever calls upon the Lord will be saved." Paul comments on this statement in Romans 10:9-13, and the terminology of Joel's text explains why Christians are described as "those who call upon the name of the Lord." Peter's speech later before the Sanhedrin will merely be a development of this same theme from Joel: it is Jesus of Nazareth, and he alone, who has received the name by which we can be saved (Acts 4:9-12). But the Pentecost speech is unusual in that it comments not only on the passage from Joel cited at the beginning, but also upon the immediate sequel in Joel which Peter had not already cited, for Peter clearly alludes in 2:39 to Joel 3:5d: "All those whom the Lord shall have called will be saved [owing to their invocation of the name of the Lord]." Thus the citation from Joel constitutes not only the starting point for the argumentation at Pentecost but also its whole background. The main point which Joel helps Peter to establish is that Jesus has become, by reason of his resurrection, the Lord whose name must be invoked by everyone who wishes to be saved on the last day.

In Peter's speech at Caesarea there is a further detail that is worth noticing: God raised Jesus from the dead "on the third day" (10:40). Mere concern for historical accuracy is not a likely explanation for this chronological notation. The Gospels tell us that Jesus himself had already taught the necessity of the Messiah's resurrection "on the third day" (Luke 24:7, 46), and Paul, repeating credal material already traditional, asserts that "Jesus rose on the third day, in accordance with the Scriptures" (1 Corinthians 15:4). Though Paul does not cite any precise Old Testament passages, it seems probable that he had some definite text or texts in mind. The Synoptics refer explicitly to the Jonah story in this connection (Jonah 2:1), discovering a typological value in his adventures: " For just as Jonah was in the belly of the whale, so will the Son of Man be three days and three nights in the heart of the earth" (Matthew 12:40). It is not excluded, however, that the Christians may also have considered another text, Hosea 6:2, as a direct prophecy of Jesus' resurrection "after three days."

Amos. The Book of Amos is quoted on two occasions in Acts, and in each case the quotation reproduces the Greek version of Amos in passages where the translation differs notably from the Hebrew original. This phenomenon is noticed elsewhere as well, and we shall soon see another example of it in connection with Psalm 16. In general it should be observed that the whole argumentation of the speeches in Acts is based upon the Septuagint text. How is this to be explained? It is insufficient to imagine that Luke was translating an Aramaic source but would turn to the Greek Bible when he encountered a quotation, for such an explanation does not account for passages in which the argumentation of the speech itself is based precisely on variant readings found only in the Greek version. We are thus led to ask whether the speeches in Acts, since they are not spontaneous compositions of Luke himself, do not directly reflect the "Hellenistic" stage of the apostolic preaching rather than its primitive Aramaic stage.

The quotation from Amos 9:11-12 in the speech of James at the Council of Jerusalem (Acts 15:16-17) is especially instructive in this regard. James wishes to show that the conversion of the Gentiles was announced and approved beforehand by God, which touches the third point of the program outlined in Luke 24:46-47. Amos, speaking of the restoration of the throne of David, promised that Israel would subjugate at that time Edom and the surrounding nations. But according to the Greek Bible, which James cites, the restoration of David's throne would entail both the renewal of the Davidic kingship and the conversion to the Lord of the remainder of mankind, of *all* nations.

Similarly, the quotation from Amos 5:25-27 in Stephen's speech (Acts 7:42-43) reproduces the considerably altered text of the Greek version. Stephen understands this passage from Amos as a reproach addressed by God to the children of Israel, who are accused of turning to idolatry in the desert. Such a reproach is a stock item in the accusations of the early Christians against the Jews: they have always been stubborn and rebellious, they constantly turned away from their God, they killed the prophets who brought them God's promises, and in the end they put to death the one who was the fulfillment of those promises (Acts 7:39-53). Thus the treatment inflicted on Jesus by the Jews is but the final act in a long history of infidelity. In this way Amos' text is made to function within a scriptural argument the purpose of which is to explain the passion of Jesus.

Habakkuk. The original text of Habakkuk 1:5 contains a threat against pagan nations, whose punishment was going to strike Israel with amazement. However, the Greek version no longer mentions the pagan nations at all; the threat is now aimed at "scorners." Paul quotes the text of Habakkuk, based on this translation, in his speech at Antioch in Pisidia and presents it as a warning meant for the Jews: if they reject his message about the Christ, they will be amazed at the consequences, at God's reaction to their attitude (Acts 13:40-41). The sequel to Paul's speech suggests that the astounding action on God's part to which Paul is alluding here is not so much a direct act of vengeance against the Jews; it is rather their displacement by the Gentiles in the economy of salvation (vv. 44-46; compare 28:26-28). Thus Habakkuk 1:5, when taken in the Greek version, also helps to demonstrate the third point of the program of Christian preaching described in Luke 24:47.

Carrying the message about Christ to the pagan nations is a task that falls in a special way to Paul. And since Paul is quite conscious of his mission, he has no trouble recognizing an allusion to himself in the passage where Jeremiah speaks about God establishing him as a prophet to the pagan nations (Jeremiah 1:5-8; cf. Acts 26:17).

The books of the Old Testament which we have been considering to this point were employed in only a fragmentary and occasional way in early Christian preaching. There are, however, two books which occupied a far more important position in the apologetics reflected in the speeches of Acts, two collections which constitute the quarry from which Christian "proof from Scripture" drew its most basic and most abundant material. They are the Book of Isaiah and the Book of Psalms. We shall consider the psalms in our third section. For the moment, we will complete our survey of the prophetic writings by considering the special contribution of Isaiah to early Christian apologetics.

The Book of Isaiah

Although the second part of Isaiah, from chapter 40 onward, is more often quoted and alluded to, nevertheless we do find in Acts one quotation from the earlier chapters of Isaiah, and a very important one at that. The text of Isaiah 6:9-10, quoted in Acts 28:26-27, constitutes the true conclusion of the entire Book of Acts. The same passage from Isaiah is also found somewhat earlier in Christian literature, of course, in the Synoptic discussion about the purpose of Jesus' parables; in that context two of the Synoptics presented a less precise paraphrase of Isaiah's passage (Mark 4:12 and Luke 8:10), but the third quoted it formally (Matthew 13:14-15). In the fourth Gospel the text is explicitly applied to the Jews of Jerusalem (John 12:40), and John's point there is similar to Paul's when he applies the text to the Jews of Rome at the conclusion of Acts: their rejection of the message of salvation has caused the Jews to become blind and hardened, but the attitude of the chosen people with respect to the Gospel should not shock or surprise us, since it is the fulfillment of prophecies. Thus the passage, Isaiah 6:9-10, is related to the same theme in early Christian preaching as the text of Habakkuk 1:5 which we considered a moment ago. The recognition of the fact that the Messiah has been rejected by Israel and that this corresponds to Old Testament prophecy leads naturally to a connected theme, the calling of the Gentiles (Acts 28:28), which is one of the proper objects of Christian scriptural demonstration (Luke 24:47).

The second part of Isaiah, chapters 40ff., which has been called the Book of the Consolation of Israel, appears in early Christian eyes as one vast prophecy about the Servant of the Lord. Needless to say the first Christians made no attempt, as many modern scholars have done, to separate and isolate the Songs of the Servant from their present literary context within the Book of Consolation as a whole. Rather they spontaneously identified the Servant with the Messiah and applied to him the totality of these chapters. But one passage must have struck them more than all the others, the great Song of the Suffering Servant (Isaiah 52:13—53:12). That text is quoted explicitly only once in Acts, in connection with Philip's preaching (Acts 8:32-33 = Isaiah 53:7-8), but the allusions that we can detect elsewhere show the profound influence of that prophecy. So familiar is it to Christians that it colors their language and they spontaneously employ its phraseology. When speaking of Jesus' "glorification," which followed upon his sufferings, they will call him "the Servant of God," alluding to Isaiah 52:13 (as in Acts 3:13, 26; 4:27, 30), or "the Just One," alluding to Isaiah 53:11 (as in Acts 3:13; 7:52; 22:14), and they regularly describe him as having been "delivered up," employing the language of Isaiah 53:12 (Acts 3:13; 7:52). All these expressions evoked the same image in the minds of the early Christians, who identify the suffering and risen Jesus with the Servant, whom the prophet presents as an innocent victim, suffering to redeem the people from their sins. Thus when Luke in the final chapter of his Gospel depicts Jesus for us on the road to Emmaus, showing his disciples through the Scriptures "that the Christ had to suffer these things before entering into his glory," we do not know exactly which Old Testament texts he is thinking of, but Isaiah 52—53 is the passage that comes immediately and most spontaneously to mind.

We believe that it is possible to detect a trace of this basic passage from Isaiah in still another place in Acts—namely in Peter's response to his interrogators (Acts 4:11). In that context Peter cites Psalm 118:22, another text that is quite familiar to the early Christians and that we shall shortly have occasion to discuss; but for the moment what interests us is simply a curious variation in the wording of that psalm as Peter cites it. The normal reading, both in the Hebrew original and in the Greek version, speaks about a stone which builders "rejected," and the rejected stone was widely recognized as a figure of Christ, but Peter speaks here about a stone that was "scorned," or treated with contempt. Now the new Greek verb which Peter thus introduces into the text of Psalm 118 also occurs in the passion prediction of Mark 9:12, a passage in which the influence of Isaiah 52:14—53:3 is clear. It would seem, therefore, that the Song of the Suffering Servant may have influenced Peter at this point too, causing him to modify slightly the wording of Psalm 118, the content and point of which are quite similar to that of Isaiah.

Another passage dealing with the Servant of Yahweh, which recurs several times, is Isaiah 49:6 in which God is said to have established the Servant as the "light of the pagan nations" and entrusted him with the task of carrying God's salvation "to the ends of the earth." This text is quite important in connection with the universal mission of the Messiah and his role as Savior of the Gentiles (Luke 24:47). It is formally quoted in Paul's speech at Antioch in Pisidia (13:47), and we can also notice its influence in another of Paul's speeches (26:23), in the words of Jesus at the opening of Acts (1:8), and, outside of Acts, in Simeon's prayer, the *Nunc Dimittis* (Luke 2:32).

Peter at Pentecost alludes to Isaiah 57:19 in close connection with Joel 3:5d (Acts 2:39), and there may be a further allusion to the same text in Acts 22:21. The passage from Isaiah is cited and commented on in Ephesians 2:13-17: Christ came to bring the message of peace not only to those who were "near," but also to those who were "far off," i.e., the pagan nations. The apologetic concern here is similar to that which we have noticed elsewhere: to justify the spread of Christianity to the pagan world by presenting that expansion as the fulfillment of messianic prophecies.

Another text from the same prophet, Isaiah 52:7, is also connected with Joel 3:5 elsewhere in the New Testament (Romans 10:5) and must also have belonged to the stock texts of the apostolic preaching. Peter alludes to it in his speech before Cornelius (Acts 10:36). The passage speaks of the good tidings (*euangelion*) of peace which God has sent to men, and Peter identifies the messenger who brings the glad news with Jesus. A few lines further on in the same speech (v. 38), Peter alludes to Isaiah 61:1, a passage that is cited explicitly in Luke 4:18: "He has anointed me to preach good news to the poor." When we read Isaiah 61:1 in its entirety, we notice that it is strikingly similar to Isaiah 52:7, for both passages speak of the glad tidings (*euangelion*), the good news of which the Messiah would be the bearer. Though reference to the good news has disappeared from Acts 10:38, we should keep that theme in our minds while reading that verse as well, if we wish fully to understand the connection between various ideas in Peter's speech. The allusion at the end of his speech to the "remission (*aphesis*) of sins" which Christ brought to all believers in accordance with the testimony of the prophets (v. 43) could also be explained as a reference to Isaiah 61:1, where the "release (*aphesis*) of captives" is mentioned; we have already seen that playing upon the various possible meanings of an ambiguous term was a popular and legitimate procedure in early Christian interpretation. Thus two texts from Isaiah form the structure of Peter's speech at Caesarea: Jesus is the messenger of peace, the Anointed One of God who came to bring men the good news of salvation.

Isaiah 59:20 is cited by Paul in Romans 11:26: "The redeemer will come from Zion, he will turn away from Jacob his iniquities." Peter may possibly be alluding to this text in Acts 3:26: "God sent his Servant to bless you, turning each of you from his wickedness." If this text from Isaiah is really in the back of Peter's mind, then the translation of Acts 3:26 which we have just given is correct, rather than the alternative translation which would be possible in itself: "God sent his Servant to bless you, provided each of you turn from his wickedness." For in Isaiah conversion is not a condition for the salvation that the Servant brings; it is identical with salvation itself.

Paul's speech at Antioch in Pisidia (13:22) recalls God's testimony in Scripture on behalf of David: "I have found in David a man after my own heart" (Psalm 89:21; cf. 1 Samuel 13:14), to which God adds, "He will do all that I desire." Now this testimony was rendered not to David, as a matter of fact, but to Cyrus, the servant of God (Isaiah 44:28). The reason Paul applies these words to David is that he considers him the figure of Christ. The correspondence between them is so close that what is said of David is eminently verified in Christ (cf. Acts 13:23), but inversely we may also apply to David what is true of Christ.

Hence, because the statement about the Servant of God is verified in Jesus, notwithstanding the fact that Isaiah was speaking about Cyrus in that passage, it may be applied by anticipation to David, the figure of Jesus. This procedure supposes that the messianic sense of Isaiah 44:28 was generally admitted. Isaiah's statement applies specifically to Jesus, whom God made Savior of Israel (Acts 13:23; cf. Romans 11:26) by raising him up (cf. Acts 5:31). God's words to David, established as king of the chosen people, apply most fully to the Christ, enthroned by God in heaven.

Stephen has occasion to quote Isaiah 66:1-2 (LXX; in Acts 7:49-50), which is a polemical text against the temple: God is the

God of the universe, and no man-made house can contain him. This polemic is closely related to the theme of the universality of the Christian message and its extension to the pagans.

Amos 9:11-12, quoted in Acts 15:16-17, treats of the same theme, and the words with which this quotation ends (v. 18) recall Isaiah 45:21, which also refers to the universality of salvation (see v. 22 as well). This is not the only case in which Luke abridges his sources while retaining sufficient elements to enable us to guess what he has eliminated; compare, for example, what remains of Isaiah 61:1 in Acts 10:38, or of Joel 3:5 in Acts 4:10-12. Hence it is not rash to consider the vague remnant of Isaiah 45:21 in Acts 15:18 as valid evidence of the use of that text as proof that in the messianic times the Gentiles, like the Jews, would be called to salvation.

The citation of Isaiah 55:3 in Acts 13:34 appears quite secondary, intended only to reinforce an argument based on Psalm 16. Isaiah's promise has been retained: "*I will give* you *the holy things* of David, the things that are faithful (or: true)," and simply juxtaposed to the verse of Psalm 16 which contains similar expressions: "You will not allow (literally: *you will not give*) *your Holy One* to see decay." This connection is purely verbal, and it is somewhat disconcerting to our sense of logic. The true, holy things of David are thereby equated with the Holy One of God, and it is suggested that God has given them by giving his Holy One not to know decay. Taken in isolation, the text of Isaiah would contribute nothing to the argument, but it is quite useful for the purpose of reinforcing the point of the psalm citation.

But what was there about this text from Isaiah that would attract attention and motivate anyone to quote it? A glance at the context may be illuminating. The words quoted above were immediately followed in their original context by the declaration on God's part: "I have made him (literally: given him as) a witness for the pagan nations, the leader and master of the pagan nations" (Isaiah 55:4). It may not be purely by accident that we should find such a statement immediately following verse 3 in Isaiah's prophecy. A Christian, reading such an affirmation in the context of the prophecies concerning the Servant of Yahweh, would naturally have interpreted it as a statement about the Messiah and his universal salvific mission. That would make it less surprising that an apparently insignificant element from the original context, such as verse 3 which is cited in Acts 13:34, should be remembered. This all gives us sufficient reason to suspect that the text of Isaiah 55:3-4 was used for apologetic purposes in the early Church.

Finally, there is an allusion in Acts 26:18 to Isaiah 42:7 (see also v. 16), which also refers to the universal mission of the Servant of God, who is destined to bring light to those who live in darkness, that is, concretely, to the pagan nations (v. 6). Paul applies this prophecy not to Jesus, but to himself. For has not the mission of bringing the light to the pagans been entrusted to him? Yet the light that he brings them is Christ (Acts 26:23 = Isaiah 49:6), and Paul is only an apostle of Christ. If the prophecy of Isaiah is fulfilled in Paul, it must first have been fulfilled in Christ. Hence Paul's use of this text in connection with his own mission presupposes its prior use for christological purposes. The message of salvation had to be announced in the name of the risen Lord to all the nations (Luke 24:47), and Paul is aware of having been entrusted with that mission in a quite specific sense.

III. THE PSALMS

David, the inspired singer of the psalms, was also a prophet in his own right (Acts 2:30). For that reason the early Christians considered the Psalter to be a prophetic collection, and they employed the psalms in their scriptural argumentation on behalf of Jesus fully as extensively as the Book of the Servant Songs.

Psalm 2 is a messianic psalm. Its opening verses mention a conspiracy of the peoples against the Lord and his Anointed (vv. 1-2), and the prayer of the apostles reported in Acts 4:25-27 illustrates how the terms of those verses were applied in detail to the narrative of Jesus' passion. Psalm 2 mentions both "peoples" and "nations," and Christian interpretation finds in the former a reference to Israel and in the latter a reference to the Romans. Among the conspirators there are both kings and rulers, allusions to Herod and Pontius Pilate respectively. And all these forces gathered together in a single place, that is, they all plotted in Jerusalem against Jesus, who is truly God's Anointed.

Verse 7 of the same psalm, "You are my son; today I have begotten you (or: I beget you)," is quoted by Paul in his speech at Antioch in Pisidia (13:33). Paul understands the statement as a prediction of the enthronement of the messianic king, and he believes that Jesus' enthronement at the time of his resurrection is the fulfillment of the prediction. Thus God, by raising Jesus from the dead, has fulfilled the messianic prophecy. A similar exegesis of this verse may be found in Hebrews 1:5 and 5:5.

Psalm 16:10 is the main element in the scriptural argument within Peter's speech at Pentecost (2:25-31) and Paul's speech at Antioch in Pisidia (13:34-37). Though Peter quotes fully four verses of the psalm (vv. 8-11), his whole line of reasoning depends upon verse 10. But to grasp its point we have to read verse 10 according to the Septuagint, in keeping with the fact we have already observed, that the scriptural argumentation of Acts is based in general upon the Greek version of the Old Testament. In the original Hebrew, the psalmist had expressed his confidence that God would come to his aid in the dangers that threatened his life: "You will not abandon my soul to Sheol, nor allow your faithful one to see the pit." He was hoping, in other words, that he could avoid being killed, that he could escape with his life. But the Septuagint translated the second half of the verse in a slightly different way: "You will not let your Holy One see corruption." Now who could this "Holy One" of God be if not the Messiah? At any rate, it is clear that the oracle was not fulfilled in the case of David, who supposedly uttered it, because David died and was buried, and his body shared the common human fate of decomposition. Jesus, on the other hand, though he also underwent death and burial, did not "see corruption," since he rose from the dead two days later. It is in Jesus, therefore, that the oracle was fulfilled, and the psalmist was speaking of him. Hence Jesus is the Messiah. Because of its dependence upon the Greek text of the psalms, it would be very difficult to date this line of reasoning any earlier than the first Greek-speaking Christian communities. Yet we believe that this argument must have been employed very early in Christian apologetics.

Peter's speech at Pentecost also contains a brief allusion to Psalm 18:6, the point of which is quite similar to Psalm 16:10. Peter asserts that, by raising Jesus from the dead, God "loosened for him the pangs of Hades" (Acts 2:24). The original Hebrew had spoken of the pangs of Scheol and the snares of death (hence the image of loosening or untying), and the psalmist had thanked God for freeing him from them in the sense of having allowed him to escape death. But Peter imagines the prayer of thanksgiving as uttered by an individual who had "seen death," i.e., actually died, and then had been brought back from death by God. The prophetic thanksgiving, understood in this way, could only be a reference to the Messiah, since whom else could the psalms be speaking about in general? Jesus, whom God raised from the dead, is undeniably the Messiah.

The Messiah had to rise from the dead. Psalm 110:1 affirms this, too: "The Lord said to my Lord, 'Sit at my right hand, till I make your enemies your footstool.'" Peter does not pass up the chance to incorporate this useful text as well into his speech at Pentecost (Acts 2:34-36). Use of Psalm 110 during the apostolic period is very widely documented, and there was no doubt about its messianic significance. It became evident, in the light of the Easter events, that if the Messiah was to sit at the right hand of God he would require his body, but without the ordinary properties of bodies. Thus God's invitation to the Messiah to sit at his right hand implies the resurrection, and the resurrection understood in its full significance as an act of enthronement. If we compare Peter's first long speech in Acts with the opening address of Paul, we notice a close similarity between the function of Psalm 110:1 as quoted by Peter and the function of Psalm 2:7 as quoted by Paul: each of these citations amounts to a messianic argument, like that from Psalm 16:10 as well, which is presented in exactly the same way.

Psalm 110:1 invites comparison with Psalm 118:16. The former represents the Messiah as commanded to "sit at the right hand of God," whereas the latter represents him as "exalted by the right hand of God" (LXX only). We find the expression from Psalm 118:16, "exalted by the right hand of God," in two passages in Acts, both within speeches of Peter (Acts 2:33 and 5:31). This prophecy, too, was fulfilled when God raised Jesus from the dead.

The messianic significance of Psalm 118 is not restricted to verse 16, however, for verses 25-26 are also messianic, and are quoted as such in the Gospels. The same is true of Psalm 118:22, the prophecy of "the stone rejected by the builders" which "became the cornerstone." This text is quoted in modified form in Acts 4:11, and also elsewhere in the New Testament. Obviously it was widely recognized as a prophecy that foreshadowed both the attitude of the Jews toward their Messiah and God's intervention in his behalf: in both of these respects it found its fulfillment in the passion and resurrection of Jesus.

In a similar context, a discussion of Jesus' resurrection against its Old Testament background, Peter recalls God's promise to David that he would put one of his descendants upon his throne (Acts 2:30). This promise is mentioned in several other passages within the Bible, such as 2 Samuel 7:12-16 and Psalm 89:4-5, but Peter seems to be influenced more directly by the language of Psalm 132:11, "The Lord swore to David a sure oath from which he will not turn back: 'One of the sons of your body I will set on your throne'" (RSV). There are two possible readings in the text of Acts 2:30. According to the shorter one, God promised David to *set* one of his descendants upon his throne; according to the longer form, God promised to *raise up* the Christ among David's descendants and set him upon his throne. The longer reading would make Peter's line of reasoning clearer, since it would be one more instance of a deliberate play upon the ambiguous Greek verb *anistemi*, which can mean both "to raise up" and "to raise from the dead." Thus the promise to "raise up" a descendant for David would have been realized concretely through the "raising up" of Jesus from the dead, which is also his enthronement. This longer reading is doubtful, however, and the shorter one, which is better attested, speaks only of God's promise to *set* a descendant of David upon his throne. Yet the choice of reading does not substantially alter the interpretation of the verse as a whole. For it was David's awareness of God's promise to him that prompted him both to predict that the Messiah would not see corruption (as in Psalm 16:10, in Acts 2:32) and to formulate ahead of time the invitation God would one day address to his descendant, "Sit at my right hand" (Psalm 110:1, in Acts 2:34). And whichever reading we choose in Acts 2:30, it is certainly in Jesus' resurrection that God's promise about the messianic king has been realized.

Acts 2:36 draws the conclusion from the scriptural argumentation that has gone before: by raising Jesus from the dead God made him both "Christ" and "Lord." In receiving the title "Lord," Jesus fulfilled the prediction of Psalm 110:1, which Peter had just cited in verse 34. Does the other title, "Christ," also correspond to a precise text utilized in Peter's argument? We find no reference to that title in Psalm 16, but we do read in Psalm 132:10 the prayer, "Do not turn your face away from your Anointed (your Christ)." Since Peter has just alluded to the next verse of the same psalm in verse 30, we may wonder whether he may have had the entire passage, Psalm 132:10-11, in mind and been influenced by verse 10 as well, even though he quotes only verse 11. Or has Luke shortened his source somewhat and dropped part of a citation, as in other cases we have seen (cf. Isaiah 61:1, in Acts 10:38)? There is still further evidence of Christian interest in the same psalm in Stephen's speech (Psalm 132:5, in Acts 7:46), though the verse quoted there serves no apologetic purpose.

Psalm 89 is similar to Psalm 132, in that it also refers to the promises that God made to David. Paul alludes to Psalm 89:21 in his speech at Antioch in Pisidia (Acts 13:22), using it as a springboard of an argument meant to establish that Jesus' resurrection was the fulfillment of prophecies. Among those prophecies, the promises that David received from God and recorded in his Psalms occupied a privileged position and attracted the very special attention of the early Christians.

Let us mention also a possible influence of Psalm 105:21 on the summary of the story of Joseph which Stephen gives us in his speech (Acts 7:10). Joseph, made leader of Egypt and of the whole house of Pharaoh, is a type of Jesus, raised from the dead by God after his sufferings and made leader of his people.

One final detail may be mentioned briefly. In his speech on the occasion of the election of Matthias, Peter quotes verses from two separate psalms as foretelling the downfall of Judas (Psalms 69:26 and 109:8, in Acts 1:20). This is only a secondary application of the texts, of course, and yet it causes no difficulty if we accept the supposition that the Scriptures had foretold the circumstances of Jesus' passion. In that case, the role of the traitor in the passion story would give him a natural place in the passion predictions.

IV. CONCLUSIONS

Our investigation into the speeches in the Acts of the Apostles has yielded a rich harvest of biblical texts. Among the texts we have discussed there are several that may escape even the attentive reader's notice on a first reading, but whose influence on the speeches may be detected by subtle traces in vocabulary and phraseology. It is not always possible to achieve certitude with regard to those implicit citations, but we hope that we have managed to keep our suggestions within the bounds of likelihood.

Several remarks of a more general nature may be appropriate at the conclusion of this survey. We offer them merely by way of suggestion, and certainly without the intention of treating exhaustively all aspects on the question of biblical interpretation in the apostolic period.

The Composition of the Speeches in Acts

Our study of the use of the Old Testament within the speeches in Acts has led us to several interesting observations about the composition of the speeches themselves. We believe that we have discovered evidence in several passages of editorial revision of earlier written source material.

One of the most striking examples of such editorial activity involves the use of Joel 3:1-5 in Peter's speech at Pentecost. Peter cites this passage from Joel extensively at the beginning of his speech (Acts 2:17-21), citing the text down as far as verse 5a. And in the course of the speech as it develops he alludes again to certain elements from that initial citation; for example, verse 33 recalls the opening verses of Joel's prophecy, and verses 34-36 seem to be an explanation of Joel's verse 5a. But then, quite unexpectedly, Peter makes a clear reference to Joel 3:5d, that is, to a verse that he has not already cited, but that follows immediately upon the portion of Joel which he did quote at the beginning of his speech. Obviously this procedure suggests that whoever composed the speech had the text of Joel in a fuller form before his eyes, and it is reasonable to suspect that the speech is a product of conscious literary activity.

On several occasions we have had the distinct impression that a conclusion was being drawn from scriptural texts which had not been quoted at all, or had been quoted only in part, prior to the conclusion. In cases of this sort we appear to be in possession of an abbreviated text that presupposes the existence of an earlier and fuller version. We have noticed, for example, that the use of the word "Christ" in Acts 2:36 is difficult to explain, but that it would be perfectly intelligible at this point if the preceding verses had quoted verse 10 along with verse 11 of Psalm 132. Again, in his speech at Caesarea (Acts 10:36-38), Peter alludes first to Isaiah 52:7 and then to Isaiah 61:1, but the connection between these two texts is not evident at first sight. To make perfect sense out of the juxtaposition, however, it is sufficient to restore the text of Isaiah 61:1 integrally, in the form in which Luke quotes it in his Gospel (Luke 4:18), for once we do that, we notice that Isaiah 61:1 has the hook-word "good news" (*euangelion*) in common with Isaiah 52:7. Further, it is quite possible that the text of Isaiah 61:1 is alluded to again at a later point in the same speech (Acts 10:43). Consequently, the form of the speech as we now have it presupposes an earlier state of composition in which Isaiah 61:1 was explicitly quoted, or supposes at least that the editor had that passage of Isaiah before his eyes.

We may also wonder whether the curious quotation of Isaiah 55:3 in Acts 13:34 does not suppose a scriptural argument based on Isaiah 55:3-4 as a whole, since verse 4 is much more significant, in fact, than verse 3. We get a similar impression regarding the allusion to Isaiah 45:12 in Acts 15:18, for the words actually cited are of little interest in themselves but they do bring to mind another text, the meaning of which harmonizes perfectly with the apologetic intent of James' speech. Recall, finally, that Peter's brief speech before the Sanhedrin (4:9-12) seems to be nothing but a paraphrase of Joel 3:5, though Joel is not explicitly cited in that context at all.

All these examples furnish evidence of editorial activity behind the speeches in Acts as we now know them. Whoever composed the form of the speeches which has been transmitted to us clearly had at his disposal written sources: either collections of scriptural citations, or else earlier written versions of the speeches which cited more explicitly and at greater length the scriptural texts on which the speakers based their comments and arguments.

Use of the Greek Bible

We should note, further, that scriptural argumentation in the speeches within Acts supposes the use of the Greek Bible. This is common knowledge, yet it is worth repeating once more, for it is a fact of considerable importance.

This dependence on the Septuagint is not the result of translation into Greek at a late stage in the composition of Acts. It would not be sufficient to maintain, for instance, that Luke made use of the Septuagint to help him translate into Greek the text of some sermons originally in Aramaic. For we have observed several passages in which the whole weight of the argument depends on readings proper to the Greek version, and in which the Hebrew text would offer no support to the argument at all. This is quite clear in the citation from Amos which James uses at the Council of Jerusalem, and in the quotation from Psalm 16:10 which is used both by Peter on Pentecost and by Paul at Antioch in Pisidia. And there are other cases in which the text as we have it makes much better sense if we presume that the speaker has the Greek version of an Old Testament passage in his mind. For instance, in the Greek translation of Psalm 110:1, the title "Lord" given to Jesus stands out far more emphatically than in the Hebrew original, because the Greek uses the same word, *kyrios*, twice ("The Lord said to my Lord. . . ."), whereas the Hebrew and the Aramaic employ two different terms ("Yahweh said to my master. . . ."). Thus the influence of the Greek Bible is undeniable in a number of cases, and quite illuminating in others.

These remarks will have bearing, of course, on our judgment regarding the historical character of the speeches. Some scholars attribute a very great role in the editing of these speeches to Luke himself, while maintaining that they are based on Aramaic sources. Others readily recognize, however, that the Christian preaching presented in Acts is so closely related to the Greek Bible as necessarily to reflect a form of preaching in the Greek language itself. We would have to acknowledge, in that case, that the speeches in Acts do not represent the apostolic preaching in its initial, Aramaic, phase, but at a second, Hellenistic, stage, which also goes back, however, to the very first years of the Church, and to the Greek-speaking part of the Jerusalem community. The importance of this group may not be underestimated, for its leaders were the seven "deacons," and it launched the great missionary movement of the apostolic period. There is also good reason to presume that Christian preaching in these "Hellenistic" circles faithfully reflected the Aramaic preaching of the "Hebrews." This fidelity was not a matter of mere mechanical repetition. Rather, the same kind of work, the theological and christological reflection which the Aramaic-speaking Christians had undertaken on the basis of the Hebrew Bible or its Aramaic translation, was also carried on once more by the Greek-speaking Christians on the basis of their Bible in Greek.

Methods of Interpretation

The fact that the preaching reflected in Acts was based upon the Greek Bible must be taken into account in any attempt to evaluate the kind of exegesis practiced in that preaching. The important question to ask is not whether the interpretations Peter and Paul give us of Old Testament texts really correspond to the *original meaning* of those texts, as we would try to reach it today by our methods of historical criticism. Our first step, when we wish to determine the meaning of a passage, is to verify its exact sense in the original language; we know we must start from the Hebrew Bible, not from the Greek version, which may be more or less faithful as a translation of the Hebrew. The apologetic speeches in Acts exhibit no such concern. Arguments are drawn directly from the Greek text, even from its smallest details, and the question whether this text corresponds with the Hebrew original never even arises.

Yet, even though the scriptural interpretation practiced in the speeches betrays no interest in the original literal meaning of the Hebrew text such as interests us today, nevertheless the speeches are also quite free of any sort of *allegorical exegesis* that would be in direct conflict with the methods of historical interpretation that we employ. Indeed, in the materials we have been considering we have not discovered the slightest trace of allegorization.

On the other hand, we have indicated several examples of

typology, though typology of a fairly simple sort that is not developed in great detail. The stories of Joseph and Moses are presented in such a way as deftly to suggest a parallelism with the passion of Jesus, but such parallelism remains discrete, scarcely perceptible, never explicit. Joseph and Moses are considered figures of Christ because of the trials they underwent and because of their salvific missions. Possibly also the emphasis given to the resurrection "on the third day" is due to the Jonah typology which is mentioned in the Gospels: thrown into the sea, Jonah saves his companions and, three days later, is himself restored to life. Finally David, whom God established as king of Israel, is a figure of the risen Christ, whom God enthrones as Lord and Sovereign Judge.

But aside from these few examples of typology, in which great men of the Old Testament function, because of the circumstances of their lives and the roles they played in history, as figures of the Messiah, early Christian scriptural argumentation adheres closely to *the letter of the text*, and even to the letter in its most material sense. We have seen that the terminology of the text itself is exploited, and on occasion even the ambiguity of the Greek vocabulary is involved, as in the case of the ambiguous Greek verb for "raising up" in Acts 3:22-26, where Peter suggests that God's promise to raise up a prophet similar to Moses was fulfilled when he raised Jesus up from the dead. Recall also the citation from Isaiah in Paul's speech at Antioch in Pisidia: "I will give you the holy things of David, the true ones" (Isaiah 55:3, in Acts 13:34), a promise that was fulfilled in Jesus' resurrection, because God then rescued Jesus from corruption, or, more literally, "did not give his Holy One to see corruption." This is an extreme case, of course, but nonetheless significant; it is an example of "literal" exegesis, quite in keeping with the practice of the rabbis.

This literal exegesis, which fixes on the slightest details of the text, is nevertheless a *messianic exegesis.* The messianic significance of the Scriptures in general can be taken for granted, and so can the interpretation given to any particular text, so that there is never any need to "prove" an interpretation in our sense of the word. Peter's reflection that the text of Psalm 16 cannot refer to David, since David died and was buried (Acts 2:29), does not constitute, to our way of thinking, a real demonstration of the messianic character of that psalm. Peter's purpose is merely to emphasize the applicability of the psalm to the Messiah, and he achieves his purpose by the striking device of ruling out a possible conflicting interpretation, namely the applicability of the psalm to the historical figure of David, an "historical" interpretation of Psalm 16 which obviously no one would find acceptable. Thus the messianic significance of texts, far from being the object of strict proof, is a postulate that no one dreams of questioning.

The point of the argumentation, therefore, is only to compare texts of uncontested messianic significance with the events of Jesus' life, or, more precisely, with his passion and resurrection. For the Old Testament is not brought to bear on Jesus' birth and infancy in Acts. Jesus' career begins effectively with his baptism by John, but there is only one speech in Acts that even speaks of Jesus' public life and ministry—namely the speech at Caesarea, in which Peter mentions the miracles that Jesus performed and presents them as the fulfillment of the prophecy of Isaiah 61:1 (Acts 10:38). Everywhere else the scriptural argumentation refers to Jesus' passion and resurrection. Its purpose is always to show that the sufferings Jesus endured and his subsequent resurrection were the object of prophecies that pointed to the Messiah, and that, consequently, Jesus really is the Messiah predicted. In addition to this fundamental theme, there is also a secondary theme, based mainly on texts from the Book of the Consolation of Israel, which is frequently encountered in the speeches in Acts: the demonstration that the salvation the Messiah brings was intended for all peoples, and that, consequently, pagan nations would be its beneficiaries. These two main points which the scriptural argumentation in Acts is meant to establish obviously correspond perfectly with the program of Christian interpretation of the Old Testament as defined in Luke 24:46-47.

This apologetic sheds a flood of Old Testament light upon the messianic events. In the light of the prophetic texts, the death and resurrection of Jesus and the preaching of the Gospel to the Gentiles take on a *theological meaning*; their significance deepens. This seems most strikingly exemplified for us in the treatment given to Jesus' resurrection within the speeches. For they present his resurrection not merely as a return to a life better than his earthly human life, but as an act of exaltation to the right hand of God, a messianic enthronement. By raising Jesus from the dead, God established him as Christ and Lord (2:36), making him the Savior (5:31; 13:23) who, on the last day, will rescue from God's wrath those who call upon his name. The christology of Acts is essentially an Easter christology because of the numerous messianic texts that shed light on Jesus' resurrection. We speak of "shedding light" because there is no question of their "proving" the resurrection in any sense. The resurrection itself is the object of the testimony of those who saw the risen Jesus, but the point of the scriptural argumentation is to illustrate the messianic character of that resurrection and to reveal thereby the deepest theological significance of Easter.

But if the Old Testament sheds light upon the Christ event, how much more light Christ sheds upon the Old Testament! Were not the texts used in the apostolic preaching all riddles before Jesus came to give them meaning? We may indeed wonder whether the ultimate significance of the Christian argumentation in Acts is not, in the final analysis, that it reveals what extraordinary light Jesus' passion and resurrection and the spread of his message sheds upon those ancient texts, *the true meaning* of which these recent events suddenly reveal! It is the Christ event itself which interprets those texts for us. There is no question in this regard of merely quibbling over individual words; rather it is all the prophecies, taken as a whole, that acquire meaning when confronted with Jesus. He gives the Scriptures meaning, he gives them *their meaning*, because he is the one who fulfills them. Scripture bears witness to the Christ, and at the same time it is he who authenticates the testimony of Scripture. The Scriptures could become fully intelligible only in the presence of the One toward whom they, in their entirety, had been all along converging.

A Table of Citations

The starting point for these reflections was the concrete examples of the use of Old Testament texts which we culled from the speeches in Acts. We hope that it has become clear that the program and method of Christian interpretation, as defined in the closing scenes of Luke's Gospel (24:26-27 and 46-47), was far from merely theoretical and abstract. The preaching of the apostolic period implemented that program concretely. And the speeches within the Acts of the Apostles give us some idea of the abundance of scriptural material the early Christian preachers exploited in that process and for that purpose.

We believe it will be useful to students if we conclude our presentation with a list which recapitulates the citations we have mentioned and explained in the course of our study:

The Old Testament		Acts
Genesis	(Abraham)	
	12:3 (18:18; 22:18)	3:25
	(Joseph)	7:9-15
	37:11, 18	7:9; cf. 3:13; 13.28
	39:2-3, 21-23	7:9; cf. 10:39
	41:40-41	7:10
	(Moses)	7:17-44
Exodus	2:14	7:27, 35; cf. 5:31; 3:13-15
	32	7:40-41
(Leviticus	23:29	3:23)
Deuteronomy	18:15, 18-19	3:22; 7:37
	21:23	5:30; 10:39; 13:29
	(David)	2:30; 13:22-23
Isaiah	6:9-10	28:26-27
	32:15	1:8
	40:5	28:28
	42:7, (16)	26:18
	44:28	13:22
	45:21-22	15:18
	49:6	1:8; 13:47; 26:23
	52:7	10:36
	52:13	3:13, 26; 4:27, 30
	52:14—53:3	4:11
	53:7-8	8:32-33
	53:11	3:13; 7:52; 22:14
	53:12	2:23; 3:13; 7:52

The Old Testament		Acts
	55:3-4	13:34
	57:10	2:39
	59:20	3:26
	61:1	10:38, (43?)
	66:1-2	7:49-50
Jeremiah	1:5-8	26:17
Hosea	6:2	10:40 (?)
Joel	3:1-5a	2:17-21, 33
	3:5a	4:9-12; 9:14, 21; 22:16
	3:5d	2:39
Amos	5:25-27	7:42-43
	9:11-12	15:16-17
Jonah	2:1	10:40
Habakkuk	1:5	13:41
Psalms	2:1-2	4:25-27
	2:7	13:33
	16:8-11	2:25-31
	16:10	13:34-37
	18:6	2:24
	(69:26	1:20)
	89:21	13:22
	105:21 (?)	7:10
	(109:8	1:20
	110:1	2:34-36; cf. 7:55-56
	118:16	2:33; 5:31
	118:22	4:11
	132:5	7:46
	132:(10)-11	2:30, (36?)

Scripture Index
of Texts Treated

161

NEW TESTAMENT